NIRVANA EXPRESS

NIRVANA EXPRESS
© 2018 by Somtow Sucharitkul
First Edition

Diplodocus Press
Bangkok • Los Angeles

ISBN:
hardcover 978-0-9900142-4-9
trade paperback 978-1940999-21-0
kdp paperback 978-19409992-5-8
ebook: 9781-940999-32-6


10 9 8 7 6 5 4 3 2 1 0

# Nirvana Express

Journal of a Very Brief Monkhood

## S.P. Somtow

Diplodocus Press
Bangkok, Los Angeles

# Contents

# NIRVANA EXPRESS

*Day Zero*

# Inner Voices

The path from birth to death is a journey without a road map.  Destinations, geography, and weather conditions are all hidden from us.  There are no signposts save those we have erected in our own minds, no tourist brochures save those we have ourselves manufactured with the tools of imagination.

This is not a story I have ever dreamed of telling.

It begins, like Dante's *Divine Comedy,* though far less poetically, in the middle of the road of life ... more precisely, the Sacramento Freeway, an endless-seeming expressway that arrows its way through the parched hills of Western California.

It   is a Friday morning in San Francisco, the morning after one of the most thrilling experiences of my career — a reception to launch my opera *Madana* in the United States.    It has been an amazing night, a artsy loft party crammed with music enthusiasts and fans as well as potential sponsors, getting to rub shoulders with opera directors and famous philanthropists — being lionized.

The next few weeks are sure to be full of exciting things.   I have just made contact with a new publisher who is enthusiastic about a possible new novel.   The British producer of a film based on my novel *Jasmine Nights* has just attached a brilliant director to the project.   There is talk of new operas, new horizons.

But an hour after I wake up that morning — on the drive home to Los Angeles — something very strange happens.   I decide to become a Buddhist monk.   Less than twenty-four hours later, I am on a plane to Thailand.   A week later, I am having my head shaved and preparing to utter the first of a string of long phrases in an ancient language I can barely understand.

No one expected this to happen, least of all myself.   I am very much a person attached to the physical world; I am deeply involved with worldly things.  I love to party.  I stay up all night discussing fine music and great literature, or pounding away at one of my computers.   I devour films, plays, and gourmet cuisine.   In fact, the notion of monks not being allowed to eat after twelve noon has always frightened me; that's about when I would normally wake up; I've always felt that if I had to live as a monk, I wouldn't be able to eat at all since I would never be awake at times when one is allowed to eat.

My lifestyle is very remote from what one thinks of as Buddhism — renunciation, detachment from desire, meditation, inward journeys. Though born in Thailand, I left when I was six months old, and was barely able to speak the language as a child; even now, I am at best semiliterate in it. In the moment that I hear the inner voice, I probably knew far more about the religions of the west — and even about Hinduism — than about Theravada Buddhism as it is practiced in Thailand.

And yet, that Friday morning, comes the inner voice. "You must go to Thailand and enter a monastery." It startles me, nodding off in the back seat of my friend Olaf's van, as we race down the freeway through the hills of California … hills the same deep ochre that you find in the robes of Buddhist monks.

I am not one to obey inner voices — or even to hear them. Yet this urge is so powerful that within moments I take out my cell phone, telephone my travel agent in Los Angeles, and book a flight for the next day. That evening, I send a fax to my parents, who live in San Francisco but are on an academic summer break in Bangkok, letting them know that I intend to become a monk.

My life has been a quest without a grail... a relentless journey from country to country, gathering data, spewing out books, sometimes to great acclaim, sometimes simply into the void ... an odyssey of sorts.  Perhaps I have finally arrived at the mid-life crisis I have been avoiding for so long. After all, at my age, I am still playing at being the *enfant terrible,* rather than the *eminence grise.* Perhaps it is time to change roles.

Truth is a sudden thing, like lightning.  I know with an unparalleled clarity that it is time to embark upon a more difficult journey, to explore that which I had never yet dared explore.

At the time, I have no clue about what Buddhist monks actually *do.*  I know that my parents will be pleased at my decision, but I don't really know why. I know that monkhood is a rite of passage that millions of Thai men, from the King himself all the way down to the poorest peasant, have gone through; that monkhood is a cultural bond that goes beyond the elaborate class system of Thai society. But I have never felt the need to be a part of that bond.

I know that monks walk around at dawn with begging bowls, but I have no idea what else they do.  I know they sit around chanting those hypnotic Pali texts, but have no concept of what the texts mean, or who wrote them.  I don't even know how one goes about becoming a monk; does one simply show up at the front door of the temple with a shaved head and a bag of robes?  Had I known, I would perhaps have hesitated. Ignorance, indeed, is bliss.

I have a friend named Sharon who lives in a mountain hideaway in Georgia. Though she seldom ventures from her home, she speaks to dozens of people daily through the magic of the internet. She is a psychic. Not a professional, in that she doesn't answer questions for money; but she is noted enough to have been asked by the police to help locate a murderer ... successfully. Sharon goes into a trance and speaks (or types into her computer) in the voice of an entity named Tomm. Twice a week, she gets together with an online group of psychics, and she has what amounts to a convention, in which people sit around at their computers channeling in tandem.

Of course, one doesn't really know whether "Tomm" exists, or whether he has been created by Sharon's own perfervid mind. And yet, whatever belief system one subscribes to, Tomm always seems to have something eerily prophetic to say. She describes his messages as extremely vivid images.

For months, Sharon has been seeing an image of me. From time to time, she has been telling me about it. It's me standing beside a lotus. The lotus keeps coming closer and closer. The lotus is, of course, a Buddhist symbol, but she doesn't know this. I have told her so, but I do not see its relevance to my life. Buddhism has been the farthest thing from my mind, until this sudden epiphany.

I decide to telephone her now, from the car. "I'm going into a monastery in Thailand," I tell her.

"I know," she says. "I saw it yesterday."

Psychics can be really smug at times.

It is Sunday midnight when I get to Bangkok, and on Monday morning I go to see a very famous Jao Khun (Venerable) at one of Bangkok's most respected temples. Since I will not disturb anyone's privacy in this memoir, I will not use the name of any monk here, and I'm not sure I'll name the temple itself. It is not one of those huge tourist temples, but it is in the heart of old Bangkok, bordered on one side by one of the few canals that still has water; other, more celebrated tourist attractions are not far, and Khaosan Road, where the backpackers gather, is a few minutes away.

Built by the most learned of all the kings of the Ratanakosin era, the temple is reached through a labyrinth of alleyways. A solitary gilded pagoda rears up above the pointed eaves, richly tiled in crimson and viridian. The Jao Khun's kuti, or dwelling place, is a few steps away from an unpretentious noodle stand; a swinging metal gate is a secret entrance to the complex. I am destined to enter the inner world through a back door.

This particular Jao Khun has gained fame as an astrologer, and so I call him the Seer. He has dedicated his life to the monkhood since his early twenties; now in his seventies, he has created quite the fiefdom within the monastic world. He has done so by obstinately refusing to accept money, unlike some other well known clerics in Thailand; when people ask to donate large amounts of cash to his charitable projects, he tells them to keep the money in their own name, letting only the interest be used for the charities. As a result, he sits atop a towering pyramid of resources, and has endowed scholarships for poor children, built Thai temples in the U.S. and Scandinavia, and has created a temple with an accompanying school for young novices outside Bangkok. As senior monks go, he is considered something of a saint.

The Seer holds court in a modest chamber; he sits on a low bed surrounded with cushions, and lined against the walls are chairs which actually appear to be recycled car seats. It's very ecology-conscious. The Jao Khun is as large and rotund as a Chinese Ho Tai or Laughing Buddha statue, and he seems to have been expecting me. "It just so happens," he tells me, "that, even though we never take in new monks at this time, your room is ready and waiting."

Since the Seer is well known for predicting the future, this should not, I suppose, surprise me. Then the Seer says, "Well, all you have to do is memorize the ritual for admittance into the monkhood — it's only a few pages long — and we're all set."

This is my first indication that becoming a monk isn't simply a matter of ringing the bell at the temple gates and shaving one's head. It seems there is a complex ritual involved, and I must formally ask, not once but three times, to be admitted into monkhood … and that I will be officially interrogated as to my qualifications by two senior monks. The language of all these exchanges is Pali, a language of ancient India.

The Lord Buddha didn't want to use Sanskrit, the language of the Hindu scriptures, as the language of his revolutionary new philosophy, because twenty-five hundred years ago this was already an ancient language. The idea of using Pali was that it was, at the time when Buddha walked the earth, a spoken language which people could immediately understand. The situation is somewhat analogous to the use of Latin in the Catholic Church up until the middle of the Twentieth Century; the Latin translation of the bible was called the "Vulgate" because it was in the vulgar tongue, that is to say, the language of ordinary people. As the centuries passed, these "common languages" became more and more uncommon. And thus it was that I found myself staring at a lengthy and enigmatic text, wondering when I would have it committed to memory enough to gain admittance to the inner world.

My next hurdle is an interview with the Lord Abbot of the Monastery, who wields great power within the walls of that world. The abbot is a stickler for tradition; he is also an extremely famous meditation guru, whose 7-day meditation course has earned him enormous attention in this country and even abroad. Here I shall call him the Guru.

The Guru is gruff at first. He complains about my posture, my manner of performing the five-point prostration, a traditional gesture of respect towards the Buddha and his living representatives; and he tells me he won't put up with becoming a monk just for a lark. "I want you to take Buddhism seriously, and I want you to enroll in my seven-day intensive meditation workshop starting on day one," he tells me.

I explain to him how the insistent inner voice sent me on this journey, and how I really know nothing at all about what I am about to experience; my mind is a blank page.

He says, "Well, such a voice could be one of your ancestors, crying out for a descendant to put on the yellow robes to ease his lot in the afterlife."

He then launches into a fascinating story about his student days in Benares. He tells me how deceased children and sages are not cremated there, but are tossed bodily into the Ganges; sometimes they float, and the birds of prey swoop down and have at them as they bob up and down in the river. "I was sitting by the river, eating my curry," he says, "when a little piece of small intestine landed — plop — right in my dish!"

Only later do I realize that this grisly tale is intended as a prelude to the formal meditation on the impermanence of the physical body.

"I've been studying the Pali text I am supposed to say," I tell him, "but I think I probably need a couple of days."

"Nonsense," the Guru tells me, "if your heart is ready, you can learn it in a jiffy." He then sets my admission ceremony for two days hence. "And by the way," he continues, "we don't pronounce our Pali the same way as in other temples. Here, we attempt to pronounce it exactly as it was pronounced during the time of the Lord Buddha himself — retroflex consonants and all."

Then, sensing my despair, he teaches me a trick for sitting in the awkward *phabphieb* position. At my age, and never having had to sit in those positions, it's weird, but to my astonishment, the guru's trick actually succeeds in allaying my discomfort for some minutes. I begin to suspect that beneath his punctilious exterior he is a compassionate soul, full of tenderness and concern.

Nonetheless, the Pali text, with its lilting rhythms and strange consonant clusters, almost makes me give up. As the dreaded day approaches, and my relatives all get in on the act, worrying about what I shall wear and who will supply the robes and begging-bowl, I become decidedly conflicted about the whole thing. I try placing the text under my pillow, thinking that perhaps I will absorb its contents while I sleep.

Just before dawn, I awaken from an astonishingly vivid dream.

I'm already in the temple in the dream, in a foyer or entrance hall, which is suffused with an incandescent light. Someone is exhuming a corpse, and when the coffin is opened I see the remains of flesh being stripped away until nothing is left but bones. And I hear a voice: "It's ready to be cremated now."

The bones are being tossed over the threshold, in a heap on the ground. Then I too cross the threshold. Inadvertently, I step on the pile of bones, and I hear the crack of a thighbone. I flinch, thinking to myself, "How disrespectful, I'm stepping on the dead."

And the voice replies, "They are nothing but old bones. They mean nothing. Let them go."

As I awaken, I realize I am no longer afraid. I have been told, with an absolute clarity, that I must incinerate the past, that I must go forth into this unknown world.

"Let them go." The dream teaches me the first and final lesson of Buddhism. The easiest to say, the hardest to put into practice. I must allow all those bones to crumble into dust … not just the fear and the emotional turmoil, but even the good things, the successes, if I am to undergo this special kind of rebirth.

And so it is that I begin the journey, leaving behind all the familiar landmarks of a convoluted life, Although it is only for a few days, I must give up all my possessions, even my identity. The time will be short, but it will encompass a life's arc of experience, from birth to epiphany to death to rebirth.

It is time. We have parked at the back gate of the temple. I am dressed in white, the color of an unwritten page, of new beginnings.

The gate begins to creak open.

# Buddhism in Thailand

To those whose knowledge of Thailand comes
from the latest exposé of the sex industry, or from
movies like *The Beach,* the idea that Thailand — and
Bangkok in particular — could be a place to look
inward, to find stillness and tranquility, might seem
contradictory.   Bangkok is a wild place, a chaotic
place, a place of legendary traffic jams, cacophonous
bars, a smorgasbord of sensuality.   To the casual
visitor, it seems quite extrovert.   It is a city so
anxious to embrace the future that it seems to bulge
at every seam.

But the places of serenity are there, and often
right in the thick of the chaos.   In fact, the serenity
and the chaos do not exist in spite of each other;
they are rather inextricably part of one another.
One must remember that, alongside the venality
that seems to pervade every corner of Bangkok's

society, there is also Buddhism, the least materialistic of the world's great religions.

In Buddhism, materialism is literally immaterial: for the entire fabric of the universe is an illusion, a dream from which one day we too may wake. That is the most basic meaning of the word *Buddha* — he who has awakened.

It's not even "an idea in the mind of God," for in its purest form Buddhism doesn't have God, or gods, at all. Buddhism doesn't affirm or deny the concept of a God or gods; it merely states that even such beings are subject to the law of causality.

When the underlying truth of the world is that it doesn't really exist at all, that is a construct that feeds upon its inhabitants' attachments, it allows you to take many more liberties with reality. That is why the recklessness and licentiousness often commented upon by those who view Thai society only from the outside, not only coexist with, but actually depend upon, religious sincerity and devout faith.

It is believed that Buddhism was brought from India to the Southeast Asian peninsula by King Ashoka, Buddhism's most famous missionary, about two centuries after the time that the Buddha walked the earth. That would be around the Fourth Century B.C., placing Ashoka's great odyssey of conversion approximately contemporaneous with Alexander the Great's conquest of India (what the Greeks called India, that is; today, this region is mostly in Afghanistan and Pakistan.)

Buddhism, then, was entrenched in Southeast Asia long before the various Thai-speaking tribes began emigrating southward from their original homeland in the Yunnan area of China.

Because Buddhism is more of a philosophy than a religion with deities to be worshipped, it easily assimilated itself into most of the cultures it touched on, oftentimes assuming forms that might have seemed strange to its founder.

The Theravada School of Buddhism, which uses the Pali language in order to remain as close as possible to the language the Buddha himself may have spoken, is now practiced only in Southeast Asia and in Sri Lanka, where the Buddhist scriptures were first written down after having been transmitted orally for several hundred years.

Buddhism permeates every stratum of Thai society and the Sangha, the community of monks, is the great leveler. The majority of Thai males do take the yellow robe at some point in their lives, even if only for a matter of days, as I did. To be a monk in Thailand, therefore, is to play a significant role within its culture in a way that is hard to achieve at one of the Thai temples in the west.

Imagine, for instance, going out with your alms bowl somewhere in North Hollywood, home to one of the largest Thai temples outside Thailand. One would soon be arrested for panhandling. A monk may not so much as heat up a bowl of soup in the microwave; he must subsist solely on food that is offered by others, and that food must be, to quote another great religious figure, "sufficient unto the day." In other words, there is no stockpiling; food that is offered must be eaten that morning. Leftovers must be distributed to others or otherwise disposed of. The food that has been left over from a monks' meal is considered "lucky" by Thais, and is often eagerly eaten.

Then, also, one would have trouble with many of the prohibitions the Sangha must dwell under — for example, not being able to even touch a person of the opposite sex. How often were Buddhist monks, traveling through Europe in the 1960s, joyfully embraced by female flower children? When I lived in Holland at the height of the hippie era, a traveling Buddhist monk told me that this was a constant source of dismay.

In Thailand, however — land of rampant capitalism and conspicuous consumption — one need never fear being misunderstood. Here, the Sangha is never far from sight ... in the dawn, receiving offerings from the pious ... rushing off to perform a quick exorcism ritual in an office building where someone has just committed suicide ... chanting at funerals, which generally last for at least seven days ... and always treated with the utmost deference.

Thailand, you see, appears to the outside world as a pyramidal society, where patronage is expected to flow from above, where the highest source of compassion and virtue is perceived to be the highest stratum of society. But the thing that stabilizes this pyramid is that there is someone to which even the pinnacle of the society, must bow. That someone is any representative of the Sangha ... any monk at all. Thus, any male person could in theory at any time experience being the very apex of the pyramid. That knowledge is what holds this madcap society together, contradictions and all.

The cop you just bribed to fix your traffic ticket, the fruit vendor you just haggled down to half-price, the waiter, the pimp, the garbage collector ... they all may once have worn the saffron robe, and been the highest mortals in the kingdom, one rung beneath the Enlightened One himself.

And that, in this nation of many inequities, is real egalitarianism.

*Day One*

# Angel who Walks the Earth

The day of the ordination is complex, and fraught with ceremony; I do not have time for doubts. An air-conditioned hall has been set up for my relatives. The Seer is nowhere to be found today; he has gone on one of his many missions to help the needy, leaving me feeling a little lost.

In the morning, I go through the Pali text I must recite. Nervous for a moment, I leave the text aside and go on the internet, where I encounter my hermit friend Sharon. She says to me, "I have a feeling that I, too, am going to the monastery. I've had a dream-vision where I was in all sorts of temples — and my head was shaven." I ask to speak to Tomm, her "entity". I type, "Will you be at the monastery too?"

"Of course," he types back. I wonder what form that will take, and whether it will terrify me. The truth is, what unnerves me most about the inward journey I must undertake is that I have always had an image of myself as a consummate rationalist. I have been able to write about the fantastic and the supernatural, indeed, made money at it. But to actually *look* into the heart of these things ... the prospect has always made me panic.

Sharon's Tomm will, it turns out, have something of a rôle to play in the unfolding story of this inward journey.

I am sitting in what will become my room — it is not exactly a cell, for though spartan, it has air-conditioning and a gorgeous antique chair inlaid with mother-of-pearl — going through the text one more time. It cannot be that hard, I keep telling myself. After all, millions of guys go through this every year.

That is, after all, one of the things I've missed out on, growing up far from the mother culture, far from the things that are taken for granted in this country. During the *khao pansa* season, the three-month "period of seclusion from the rains," young Thai men everywhere become monks, pledging to remain for the duration of the season. Are these men impelled by inner voices? Perhaps. Tradition tells us that a man's duty is to seek the yellow robe for a time, in order that his parents may be reborn in a celestial realm. Perhaps there is some pressure from elders involved. Perhaps it's simply the thing to do. This is not a decision that can be forced on a person, however, which is why a monk-to-be must ask — three times — in an ancient tongue — to be admitted into the Sangha. And although the decision is, indeed, reversible, and one can leave far more readily than one can join, the words of the ceremony contain frequent references to "the rest of one's life."

The Guru has told me that he won't accept a three-day monkhood — although I am later to learn that one of the new monks did in fact leave on the third day, unable to handle things — or even a seven- or nine-day monkhood. "This isn't a holiday," he said to me. "You must actually embark upon a real voyage toward the truth. I will allow you to remain here only if you do so for a minimum of fifteen days. After all, His Majesty the King himself, despite all of the affairs of state, was able to sacrifice fifteen days of his life to live among the Sangha. You can do no less."

Fifteen days, then, or a little longer, since the time of leaving a monastery must be accurately defined, to the exact minute, by reference to astrological charts, is the time I shall be within these walls. This will be the fast track, the express train to self-discovery.

A *Maha,* who has been a monk for fourteen years and is an excellent drill sergeant, helps me. He is a small man, slender, very delicate in his movements; my mother mistook him for a *samanera,* one of those young boys who often take up the yellow robe for a while and who are asked to observe only ten precepts rather than the 227 that monks must obey. She was astonished to discover that he is already working on his master's degree at the Buddhist University. The Maha has been ordained since the age of twelve.

The Maha sits on the mother-of-pearl inlaid chair in my room, acting the role of the Upajjhaya who will accept me into the monastery. I manage to get through the text, if haltingly, and he smiles. "Don't worry about a thing," he tells me. "A lot of people botch it up far more than that. And if you stumble, someone will prompt you."

So much for my fear of flunking the entrance exam.

Since the ordination is to take place at 4:15 p.m. my family is afraid that I will starve to death afterwards — because, you see, a monk may not eat after noon. And this temple is very strict; some sects would consider, for example, a banana in a blender to be a drink, not food, but here it is a no-no. So, there is the obligatory last meal — quite a feast really, for there is a hole-in-the-wall restaurant down the street that is famous throughout Bangkok for its moist, firm-textured roast duck.

On a balcony that separates two residential sections of the kuti, I sit in a plastic chair while the Maha supervises the shaving. There is ceremony involved here, too. Once one has become a monk, one may not touch a woman — the lightest tap is considered an *apatti,* or offense, and entails ritual purification — but the cutting of the hair is always begun by the senior female relatives — first my mother, then assorted aunts. The scissors are a little rusty — no one thought of bringing a pair from home — but once the first cuttings are collected into a glass bowl, later to be laid on the family shrine, the Maha continues the job with a sharp razor. He's clearly used to doing this; in no time at all I'm completely bald. The eyebrows too, of course.

I take a look in the mirror. I am not yet a monk, and monks are not supposed to look in mirrors.

"What about shaving?" I ask, alarmed.

"You can look at a mirror for that," the Maha tells me, "because that's a practical reason. You just can't go staring into mirrors for the purpose of admiring yourself, or beautifying yourself. That would be *apatti.*"

It is also, it seems, an *apatti* to wear black sandals, and the previous day we have hastily purchased a pair of brown ones from the nearest department store.

Out of nowhere comes a torrential monsoon shower, which just as suddenly ends. The sky continues to be overcast. A moist wind blows. These are good omens for an ordination.

Now it is only an hour before the ceremony. I put on a white dress shirt, and around my waist I wear a large white piece of fabric that resembles a tablecloth; it folds back and forth in the front and then is tied with a sash-like belt of the same material. It is a sort of sarong. Monks, I am dismayed to discover, do not wear underwear.

The waiting room has begun to fill with relatives. Even though the decision to become a monk was sudden, and I only told my parents, word has begun to leak out. A *Buat Naak* ritual is not unlike a bar mitzvah. There are the beaming parents, the fussing aunts, and the bar mitzvah boy sweating over whether he's going to screw up the chanting. There is a table laden with offerings, for all the monks who officiate at the ceremony must receive gifts of the prescribed type.

And now I put on over my white garments a lace and gilt surplice. It is because of this stunning piece of embroidery the pre-monk outfit has come to be known as the "angel who walks the earth" costume. Wearing it, one does feel remarkably angelic. As if one is clothed in light. I try walking a few steps. I even feel lighter, more ethereal.

My aunt has readied a tray of coins, which I will, before crossing the threshold of the chapel, cast out onto the pavement, symbolizing my rejection of the material world.

And now we emerge from the waiting room. There is to be a ritual promenade around the chapel, three times, clockwise, the candidate for monkhood in his glittering gold and white apparel leading the way, the relatives following. It is a beautiful chapel, the stone of the walkway worn down, indented from a hundred years of such processionals. We do not proceed in straight lines as there is an occasional pile of doggie-poo to circumnavigate. Buddhist temples do not deny protection to *any* needy souls ... always, there are the stray dogs. Later, I will learn that even faeces have their place in the monks' daily contemplation of the impermanence of the universe.

At the threshold, I pause for a moment. With one gesture I fling away all the coins in the tray. Later I learn that I was supposed to sprinkle them hither and thither, but it seemed somehow more right for me to cast off all venality at once.

Then, my mother carefully grasps the hem of my angel surplice. Each of the relatives holds on in turn, so that we become links in a chain of humanity. This symbolizes the fact that I will dedicate all the karmic merit of my monkhood to others, who will climb to heaven by clinging to the edge of my robe.

And so it is that I step inside the chapel, and am face to face with the earthly representatives of the eternal dhamma, the law of cause and effect that governs the cosmos.

Beneath a tall image of the Buddha seated in meditation, there are about fifteen monks. Some I know: the Guru is there, as is the Maha. Others I will come to know. Prostrating myself three times before this august body, I begin to chant, in Pali:

*Reverend sir,*
*I go for refuge unto that exalted one,*
*Though he has long since attained nirvana....*

I am kneeling, holding a set of robes in my forearms, as I struggle through two pages of text; occasionally the Guru intervenes to correct my pronunciation. It is not kind to my arthritis, especially once it is over, for the Guru proceeds to preach a mini-sermon.

"The Buddha," he says, "actually existed. He actually did achieve Enlightenment. You would not be here unless you believed these things."

At length, he commands me to depart, and in the corridor outside the chapel, several monks help me to change from the angel costume into the simple ocher robes of monkhood.

Alas, they are not that simple. The outer robe is a rectangular piece of cloth, but the human body is not a rectangle. Later, I will practice, and practice, and practice, but for now, it takes three monks, and another to hold my arm in place, and yet another to tie the thing down with a length of saffron cloth to prevent it from undoing itself in the midst of the proceedings.

I return, feeling a little self-conscious. I prostrate myself before my parents, because I am bidding farewell, in a very real sense, for all time; when I return to the world, I will not be the same person, I will have been reborn.

And then it is my parents' turn to present me with my begging bowl, and to prostrate themselves before me, for I am no longer their son, but a living embodiment of the dhamma, in an unbroken chain of discipleship that extends twenty-five hundred years back into the past, to the ones who first sat at the feet of the Enlightened One himself.

I am interrogated, twice, in the Pali language, about my qualifications for the Sangha. Am I a leper? Am I exempt from military service? Am I a fugitive? Most people answer these yes-no questions by simply remembering that the first five are *natthi bhante* (no) and the rest *ama bhante* (yes). Since I have worked from a romanized text that has an English translation, I have the advantage of understanding what has been asked.

By now, my aging body is a wreck from having wrenched itself so long into the formal position of respect. The Guru, sensing my discomfort, tells me, "Well, it's done; you're a full *phra* now. But I must recite the *Anusasana*, the words of instruction to the new monk. It will take about five minutes. Instead of kneeling all the way down, you can sort of stand on your knees, if you like."

He then races through this lengthy Pali text with Donald Duck-like celerity. I am amazed at how he can memorize so much and say it all so quickly, missing nary a beat. My gratitude is as boundless as my excruciation. And afterwards, with much snapping of photos and presenting of offerings to the temple, I emerge from the chapel, ready for the next stage of the journey.

Finally, I am alone in the room. I know that I may not eat until dawn, but for some reason there is no hunger at all. It is something to do with the yellow robe I am wearing. I do not feel the same, but as yet I have no clue as to what will happen next.

At around seven o'clock, the Maha shows up with a small ceremonial tray with candles, a small arrangement of flowers wrapped in a banana-leaf cone, and a glass of water.

"You must go now," he says, "and formally present yourself to your Upajjhaya, the abbot."

I move through empty courtyards in the gathering night. The air hums. Here, in this crowded metropolis that teems with noise and pollution, though I do not know who I am and where I am going, I feel strangely free from care.

There is a brief interview with the Guru. He insists that I sit in the *phabphieb* position, with my palms folded in supplication, which is the proper deference to show one's guru.

He says to me, "Well, you made it through the ceremony. For someone who has spent his whole life abroad and can barely read Thai, even that is an accomplishment."

I thank him for speeding through the Anusasana, but he brushes off my gratitude, presenting me instead with a pile of books which he wants me to read in a certain order. Many are in English; most have been written by the Guru himself. "Normally," he said, "I would require you to render daily services to me as your guru, such as washing my robes, and bringing me water to drink in the evenings; however, since we are not living in

the same kuti, I shall not ask that of you; only that
you read the books. Now, return to your abode and
rest." Abruptly, the interview is over.

It is only eight o'clock, but I feel extremely worn
out after a day that began at five in the morning. As
I lie down, though, not quite daring to remove my
robes for fear I may never be able to put them back
on again, there comes a knock at the door.

It is a monk I do not recognize. He says, "The
abbot requests that you go to the *vihara* to practice
meditation with the other meditation students," he
tells me. "You won't have any idea what is going
on, but he wants you to go along with whatever's
happening, try to get the hang of things."

Once more, I set off into the night. And it really
is night; the sounds of the city seem immeasurably
distant as I cross the courtyard, pass one pagoda,
traverse the grounds of the chapel where I was
ordained, and enter, through a worn wooden portal,
an inner world within the inner world. A cloister,
completely lined with life-sized standing Buddha
images, surrounds a central atrium from which rises
a gilded pagoda.

A dozen women, dressed in white, are walking
back and forth in the cloister with great
deliberation, staring at the ground, measuring each
step. They are, I assume, meditation students.
When they see me, or rather, when they see my
yellow robes, for I have not yet found the "me"
inside those robes, they bend low, place their palms

reverently together; I am unused to such obsequy; it is yet alien to me.

Carefully, I go up the steps to the great *vihara*. Inside, a great image of the seated Buddha towers over dozens of others; there are images of Thai kings, of holy men turned to face the great teacher; the columns are intricately painted with floral motifs and panels depicting the Buddha's life, and every inch of the walls is covered with images from the Jatakas, the tales of the Buddha's previous incarnations. There is a whiff of incense in the air. There are grandfather clocks on every wall, and not a single one is synchronized to any other; constantly, they jangle. Time has no meaning here.

Columns set off an upper platform where monks are sitting on padded squares of cloth. They all seem to know exactly what they are doing. One motions me to sit beside him.

There comes a voice on a loudspeaker: "We will all now sit in meditation for twenty minutes."

I cannot achieve a partial, let alone a full lotus position; I wriggle as I try to warp myself into what seems to have come so naturally to the other monks. They sit, hands resting on their laps, eyes closed, gazing at some inner center; while for the next twenty minutes, a seeming eternity, I struggle with aching joints and nervous tension. I know I'm supposed to do something with my breath; I try different things; but I all can feel is the pain.

*Fifteen more days of this?* I ask myself. What of the glorious hero on his quest? Will I just end up wallowing in arthritic agony?

I try to think of my comfortable bed at home in Los Angeles, complete with 300-channel digital cable, climate control, huge DVD library, instant internet access, and thirty-minute home delivery of any ethnic cuisine. The strange thing is, the memories refuse to surface. I want to ask my inner voice why I was sent here, but those inner voices never answer when you want them to.

I grit my teeth. Next time, I will remember to apply the muscle relaxant spray and rub in some ointment before venturing forth to meditate.

When fighting the dragons of career and love in the world outside, one expects a little exhaustion. I am now learning that the journey within, too, is not without physical torment.

But then again, tomorrow is another day.

# The Ordination Ceremony: *the script*

It is remotely possible that some readers of this memoir will, as I did, feel a sudden urge to rush off to Thailand and become Buddhist monks. This is not quite as strange as it sounds. Many westerners have found profound satisfaction in spending time in a Buddhist monastery, and Thailand's hundreds of temples have seen their share of "farang" monks, many of whom have been exemplary representatives of the dhamma.

For a head start on learning the Pali text, here is the entire ritual, including something many Thai language manuals of instruction leave out completely — a translation.

Approaching the company of the Sangha on his knees, and carrying a set of robes on his forearms, the supplicant places the robes on his left, proffers the tray of offerings to the Upajjhaya, prostrates himself three times, kneels, lifts up the robes once more in his forearms, and, his hands joined, speaks:

> *Esaham bhante, suciraparini-*
> Reverend Sir, I go for refuge
> *buttampi, tam bhagavantam*
> to that Exalted One, though he has
> *saranam gacchami,*
> long since attained Nirvana,
> *dhammañca bhikkusakhañca.*
> along with the Dhamma and the
> Company of the Bhikkus.
> *Labheyyāham bhante,*
> Reverend Sir, may I receive
> *tassa bhagavato,*
> the Exalted One's
> *dhammavinaye pabbajjam*
> Going-Forth in the Dhamma-Vinaya;
> *Labheyyam upasampadam*
> May I be granted Acceptance.

As is always necessary with such formulae, the above is spoken three times. The second time, the first word is replaced with dutiyampāham (for the second time, I...) and the third time with tatiyampāham (for the third time, I....)

The supplicant continues:

> *Aham bhante, pabbajjam yacami.*

Reverend Sir, I beg for the Going-Forth
*Imāni kāsāyāni vatthāni gahetvā,*
As I have taken these yellow robes,
*pabbajetha maṃ bhante,*
Grant unto me the Going-Forth
*anukampaṃ upādāya.*
In your compassion for me.

This formula is also spoken three times, the second and third time prefaced with the words *dutiyampi* and *tatiyampi*.

The Upajjhaya accepts the robes, places them in front of himself, and then gives the monk-to-be instructions in the basic knowledge of the Buddha, Dhamma, and Sangha, and the benefits of ordination. This mini-sermon is not preset, so be prepared to kneel for a while. You might want to practice at home.

The pep talk culminates with a discussion of five "unpleasant" body parts, which the Upajjhaya will name in Pali and which the monk-to-be should repeat:

*Kesā, lomā, nakhā,*
hair of the head, hair of the body, nails
*Dantā, taco*
teeth, skin

These are subjects for meditation. Once this is done, the Upajjhaya places the shoulder-cloth from the set of robes, places it on the supplicant's shoulder, and hands him the rest of the robes.

The supplicant retires to another part of the chapel, and puts on the robes, generally with assistance from more experienced monks.

When he comes back, in saffron-robed splendor, the monk-to-be kneels once more. Another elder bhikku, an ajarn or teacher, presides now, and the supplicant must request that he be granted the three refuges and ten precepts of a novice.

*Aham bhante saraasîlam yacami.*
Reverend sir, I beg for the refuges and precepts.
  *Dutiyampi aham* etc.
  A second time, I ...
  *Tatiyampi aham* ... etc.
  A third time, I ...

The ajarn then recites the three refuges and ten precepts, which the monk-to-be repeats, line by line. Since this does not have to be memorized by the monk, I will just explain briefly that the three refuges (recited thrice each) state that the monk goes to seek refuge in the Buddha, the Dhamma, and the Sangha. The ten precepts (a forerunner of the 227 that a full-blown monk must obey) are four of the five commandments that all Buddhists are supposed to follow — refraining from taking life, taking what is not given, speaking falsehood, indulging in intoxicants, with the one about sexual improprieties being rephrased to mean complete celibacy. Then there are five, rather more severe commandments: refraining from dancing or singing or other such amusements, refraining from eating after twelve noon, refraining from makeup and adornments, refraining from sleeping in high or wide beds, and refraining from touching gold and silver (that is to say, any kind of money whatsoever).

Once the ordinand has repeated all those phrases, he is a samanera or novice. Boys who ordain as novices only have to get this far and they're all done; monks-to-be have a further process to follow. They must ask for nissaya, that is dependence — to have the Sangha and the Upajjhaya as their sole support.

*Ahaṃ bhante nissayaṃ yacami*
Reverend sir, I beg for dependence.
*Dutiyampi ... etc.*
For the second time, etc.
*Tatiyampi ... etc.*
*Upajjhayo me bhante hohi,*
Be my Preceptor, reverend sir!
                    (three times.)

The preceptor says yes (or one hopes he does) in various ways, to which the correct answer is invariably *Sādhu bhante.*

You then say:

*Ajjataggedāni thero mayhaṃ bhāro,*
Henceforth I shall bear the Thera's burden
*Ahampi therassa bhāro.*

And I shall be the burden of the Thera.

This is followed by three prostrations.

The Upajjhaya then informs the novice that it's
time to ordain him into the Dhamma-Vinaya, the
discipline of monkhood. He tells the ordinand what
his name will be in Pali (this has been carefully
figured out beforehand, by matching the
supplicants given name with its closest possible
meaning in Pali as well as considering such
auspices as what day of the week he was born on)
and then he tells the novice the Pali names of the
distinctive emblems of his monkhood, the alms
bowl, the various robes, and so on; to each of these
instructions, the novice responds *āma bhante*, which
by now you have figured out means "Yes, reverend
sir." The ajarn then informs the assembled monks
that he is going to examine the applicant — all, of
course, in Pali.

The novice backs off to another area of the
chapel, where a small rug has been placed on the
floor. The ajarn then, standing on the rug, after duly
exhorting the novice to tell the truth (in Pali) begins
to question him. The first five questions are about
diseases: he asks if you're a leper, an epileptic, and
so on, to which the correct response is *natthi bhante*.
There follow a series of other questions —
including, oddly enough, whether you are a human
being (on the off chance that you may be some
demon in disguise) and "are you exempt from

military service?" — no draft-dodgers here! — to all of which one must respond: *āma bhante.* Then follow two questions which actually require some thought: "What is your name?" at which one must actually remember to insert the Pali language name one has just been given into the sentence: *Aham bhante (name) nāma.* Next, one is asked the name of one's Upajjhaya, to which the response is: *Upajjhāyo me bhante āyasmā (name) nāma.* In this particular case, remembering one's own name can be a bit of an ordeal, but someone will probably remind the novice.

There's a bit of give-and-take now between the assembled monks and the Upajjhaya, and then — it may come as some relief — the monk-to-be has one last bit of Pali left to memorize: he must request acceptance.

*Sanghambhante upasampadam yacami.*
Reverend sir, I beg for acceptance.
*Ullumpatu mam bhante,*
May the Sangha, in its compassion
*Sangho anukampam upādāya,*
raise me up.
*Dutiyampi bhante, sangham upasampadam,* etc.
*Tatiyampi,* etc.

Here the trick is that in the second and third time, the word order changes a little bit, because elegant Pali syntax requires that the word *bhante* be the second idea in the sentence. Always something to keep the hopeful monk on his toes.

From this point, there is nothing else to remember. There is a second "questioning", but it's exactly like the first, except it's in a kneeling position rather than a standing one. Then, there's a lot of chanting back and forth, where the Upajjhaya informs the Sangha that the examination is complete; the monks then get a big chunk of chanting in unison. Then, there is the five-minute admonition, to which one responds (in Pali) "yes, reverend sir"; then more chanting, during which the now fully ordained monk pours water into a little bowl. This represents the fact that he is allowing all the good karma of his ordination to be given to his ancestors.

After all this, there are offerings to be presented, and — about ninety minutes from the first prostration — it's time for the photo-op.

It's a breathtakingly beautiful ritual, and one considerably more meaningful if one knows what is being chanted — by no means always the case.

*Day Two*
# Walking Meditation

The second day of my monkhood, I rise even earlier than the 5 a.m. "official" wakeup time. There is no bell, no alarm; a Thai monastery doesn't operate by enforcing time constraints. People are expected to get up of their own volition. I do have an alarm clock, but I don't use it today.

I then spend about an hour trying to put on the robes.

One might think that it can't be that difficult to get a yellow bedsheet to stay put, but it's quite a process. The robes come in various sizes, and the Seer has ordered a large one for me, since I've got a bit of a paunch. But it's decidedly long, and wrapping in becomes rather unwieldy.

You see, the first thing is that there is, in fact, an inside and an outside to this contraption. You can tell from the seams, for a robe is stitched together from precisely 32 pieces of cloth, which symbolize the 32 unpleasant parts of the body which are used for the meditation on the impermanence of the human form.

In ancient times, robes were literally made from castaway material, even dead people's shrouds, sewn by the monks themselves and then dyed this simple yellow for the sake of uniformity. Some of the 227 regulations for monkhood include detailed instructions about the needle cases monks may possess, what materials they may be made from, and so on. These days, with robes being off-the-rack, as it were, the regulations are seldom cited.

You must envision me, alone in my room in this strange place, learning all over again, in my late forties, how to get dressed. I am like a toddler, helpless, but I struggle. First, you find the little square of sewn cloth that tells you where your neck goes, thus making sure the robe is on right-side-up and not inside-out. Then, you wind it around yourself — not symmetrically, but the left side *over* the shoulder and the right side *under*. You join the ends, and begin twirling them together, much as you might roll a poster into a mailing carton. Grabbing the top end of this roll, you hold it as high as you can with your left hand; then, you wrap a flap that seems to appear out of nowhere over your left shoulder and around the arm. Then, bunching up the twisted roll with your right hand, you twirl it some more, at the same time lifting it to make sure the hem of the robe clears the ground. You then toss the twirl over your left shoulder, catch the end in the left hand, and pull, so there is a sort of handle under your arm with which the robe can be tightened, hitched up a little, and otherwise prevented from falling off.

There is a prize for anyone who understood the preceding paragraph.

I do not understand it myself, nor am I certain I will ever accomplish what it describes in my short time here.

All I know is that I spend something like two hours experimenting with the robes, and by the time I descend to the Seer's audience-chamber (which is also his breakfast nook) I still haven't figured it out, and must humiliatingly ask for help from the Littlest Novice, a 13-year-old Southern kid with a disarming smile.

Over breakfast, the Seer tells me how he became a monk, but I am still in a sort of miasma. Sometimes I don't understand what he says. "In my youth, I became a monk in front of a waterbuffalo," is what I keep hearing, but it's because the Seer still has a trace of a provincial accent, and he's really telling me he became a monk "before the flames" — he was referring to the custom of entering the monkhood to honor a dead ancestor at a cremation ceremony, the monkhood lasting only as long as the funeral pyre itself. It is with great confusion that I hear his tale while attempting to eat rice gruel with the decorum that is required of a monk — chewing loudly, with one's mouth full, and other impolitenesses are all against the 227 regulations of monkhood.

The Seer's tale continues. He tells of having two options in his youth: the monastery or the military. He decided on the monastery, way down in the remote rural South of Thailand, and after a while, his preceptor tempted him with an offer: if he could pass his religious exams, he would send him to Bangkok. "Bangkok, in those days," says the Seer, "might have been an alien planet. Boy, I sure wanted to see the big city. And it turned out, I was the only one to pass the exam."

Eating breakfast as a monk — my first real meal as a monk — is quite an experience. There is a lady who keeps presenting us with food as the conversation progresses, but I may not receive food from her directly because she is a woman; I must first place a yellow cloth on the table, and, holding on to one edge with both hands, allow the dish to be placed upon the cloth; I then place the dish with the others and am free to partake of it. Alas, if the lady should accidentally touch the dish after I have already received it, she must present it properly all over again.

I expect morning chapel (my first experience of chapel as a full-fledged monk) to be as taxing on the knees as the ordination ceremony, but it is mercifully short. As a monk, I can't hide in the very back, sidling up to the wall to rest my weary back; I have to take my correct place, which is in fact as the very last monk in the very last row of monks, yet not as far away as the novices, of which there are about two. To my relief, chapel is much shorter than I think.

Everyone stares because I'm peering at an English-language chanting manual, with transcriptions of the text. A senior monk up front begins with a little intro, and we're off, chanting our way through the praises of the Buddha, Dhamma and Sangha, pausing now and then to fall to the floor in the five-point-prostration, a very precise positioning of the body so that the knees, elbows, palms, and forehead are all perfectly aligned in a sort of pyramid.

Then, with barely a ten-minute break, comes a full morning's worth of meditation. The Guru is in the midst of a running a seven-day intensive meditation workshop, and now, it seems, I am to learn the meaning of some of the things I was attempting the previous night.

When I arrive, the main vihara is crammed with eager meditators. All are dressed in white, all but one monk, who looks almost as old as me, and decidedly as uncomfortable. He is seated on the upper platform, leaning against one of the square columns, ornately frescoed with decorative floral motifs against a lapis-blue background. He turns to smile at me, and I realize that this, too, is a new monk; there are rumors that among the crop of young monks, there is another my age, who, like me, has decide late in life to begin his inward journey.

"So," he whispers, as I crawl up the steps of the stone platform and seat myself on a flat yellow cushion in the monks' area, "I am not alone anymore — there'll be two of us aging monks struggling our way through this ordeal."

"Are you all right?" I whisper.

"Well, this sitting position is hard to take," he says. "I'll have to remember my muscle relaxant spray tomorrow." My thoughts exactly.

I will refer to this new old monk as the Thinker, because later it will transpire that he is constantly analyzing the teachings of the various gurus in the temple.

I turn to the images of the Lord Buddha and perform the prostration to the Triple Gem. The Guru is already seated on his preaching chair, facing the meditation students who are clearly in awe of him. I have arrived a little late, and the lesson is in full swing. To my astonishment, even though the students are sitting very still, very respectfully, and without seeming to strain to maintain their *phabphieb* position, this is not a somber group at all. The Guru is telling them about controlling the breath, interlacing the rather dry narrative with anecdotes about India, many of which seem to have to do with either excrement or body parts.

The Guru instructs us to breathe slowly and rhythmically, to use the sound of the word *buddho* as a focus: *bud* for breathing in, *dho* for breathing out.

*Buddho* of course is a Pali word, a title of the Buddha, and it essentially means "he who is awake." *Awake,* so much more homely a word than *enlightened,* is perhaps closer to the original sense of what Buddhism is about: seeing past illusion.

It is only nine in the morning, but I have been awake since four — in itself a startling innovation, as I have risen before my customary bedtime. The light that streams into the vihara from windows, bordered by gilded shutters with fading gold leaf designs, is bright, warm; the heat that suffuses the vihara is intermittently mitigated by standing electric fans that turn this way and that, an incongruous intrusion of technology.

And now, the moment of truth: we are to meditate for twenty minutes. I try the *buddho-buddho* thing several times, but it is, to say the least, abortive. I begin to fidget. I open my eyes a few times, and it reminds me of a certain episode of *The Twilight Zone* — wow, this is really dating me, isn't it? I mean the one where (if memory serves me) the character ends up trapped in a space-time warp where time is moving a million times faster for him than other people, so they all seem to be statues to him, and is a blur to them....

How to find the inner stillness?   It does not come.

The jangling of a dozen unsynchronized grandfather clocks tells me that it is now long past eleven o'clock, the lunchtime of monks, and that the magic hour of twelve, after which no solid food may pass a monk's lips until dawn of the next day, is fast approaching. When we emerge from our meditative state — well, when *they* emerge, for my state has been that of bewilderment — it is 11:30, and naturally I'm starting to get worried — especially when the Guru immediately launches into one of those numerical expositions that seems to be such an important feature of the more theoretical aspects of Buddhism. What I mean by these numbers is this: there are groups of ones, twos, threes, fours, and so on: four types of *brahmavihara,* eight sides to the *eightfold* path, and so on: I could show you an entire book of numerical lists.

The Indians have always been masters of lists. As a musician, I am astonished that only Indian music has divided the octave into 66 divisions or *srutis,* while poor old Western music has a mere twelve, and Thai or Indonesian music even fewer. The Buddhist scriptures, which came from India, have more lists than you can shake a stick at. I think that the lists are important to those who are in love with lists, but perhaps, for those who wish to journey to the heart of Buddhism without stopping to admire the view on the way, the Four Noble Truths might be enough.

As the expounding of lists proceeds, my friend the Thinker turns and whispers to me, "I think we'd better prostrate ourselves and leave, or we'll miss lunch."

The Lord Buddha did not believe in self-torture. Indeed, after tormenting himself in fakir-fashion for some time in order to try to attain enlightenment, he realized that mortification of the flesh wasn't the way to the truth, and began eating and drinking like a normal human being. He was much reviled by his associates for this; but later on he convinced them that his was the right path, and they, too, ate.

In my own small way, then, I am reliving this significant episode in the life of the great Teacher.

We prostrate ourselves to the Guru (who, being deeply involved in his exposition, barely acknowledges our departure) and make it to the lunch pavilion *just* within the threshold. Having seated ourselves and begun, we are safe from *apati*. But there is some ceremony yet, for this is a lunch that is being presented to us by the faithful, and some other monks have kindly joined us to keep us company — all of them new monks — fresh boyish faces, unlike my companion and myself.

To my wonderment, I discover during lunch that I'm no longer this writer-composer with the millstone of celebrity hanging around my neck. Along with my hair have gone many other outward trappings of my life. The young monks question me about America and about why I have to follow the chanting with a romanized textbook, but they do not know anything about me. And this is very liberating. It is actually possible, at this late stage in my existence, to become once again an unwritten page, a born-again virgin.

After the lunch, I brace myself for another session of wrenching sitting positions and useless meditation, but it then occurs to me that the Guru *did* tell me the previous evening that some people do meditate in chairs. I wonder whether I should interrupt the abbot's lecture to ask him for permission to do so.

Then, in a flash of understanding, it occurs to me that this isn't like being at boarding school in England. No one is making me torment my muscles. No one has forced me to become a monk. If I get up, and stagger over to one of the many chairs that line the outer vestibule of the vihara, no one will try to stop me, nor will I be summoned to a stern lecture from some bespectacled schoolmaster brandishing a cane.

It's another liberating moment. Not that it would do to just get up and stalk off to a chair. A monk must be gentle and reflective in his movements, must not raise his voice or attract attention to himself. So I sort of unobtrusively slither, while still in a sort of semi-prostrate position, behind a huge green frescoed column, feeling somewhat like an overweight caterpillar as I do so.

The chairs are these one-piece plastic things, the stackable kind you find at picnics and beaches. Their very homeliness, amidst the massive gold Buddhas and the brilliant primary colors of the murals, are a reminder of the vainglory that underlies the splendid edifices we have built for ourselves.

This would be an uncomfortable chair back in my world of L.A. conveniences, but suddenly it is the greatest blessing on earth to be relieved from the physical contortion of the lotus position.

At that moment, the Guru begins an oration about Nirvana. He says something that makes me sit right up. "Nirvana isn't necessarily something remote, something that you will never achieve at all in this life. There is the great Nirvana, the complete and permanent cessation, the utter peace that has no boundary … but there are also momentary Nirvanas … brief glimpses of the great Nirvana. Do not forget that. Those brief glimpses can come at any time, and they are just as valid, for time and space are themselves illusion, and a moment can be eternity."

This is a startling revelation to me. I have always believed that Nirvana is a sort of theoretical, unattainable pot of gold at the rainbow's end; that one's lot in life is to be aware of the rainbow at least, and not to worry to much about the destination. I resolve to close my eyes and try for such a fleeting glimpse, but all around me, I hear the sounds of people getting up from their various sitting positions.

It is time to practice another style of meditation, called *jongkom* in Thai, *cankama* in Pali.

Basically, this means walking around.

Well, back home, we've all walked for AIDS, we've marched for dimes and other noble causes; why not walk for self-illumination? The Guru begins to regale us with the five (yes, another list from India!) benefits of the walking meditation. One of these benefits is improved performance of the digestive tract. You see, Buddhism, unlike many western religions, cares about such things as regularity in bowel movements.

I am, as a typical product of these harried times, of course rather skeptical that walking can lead to *piti,* a state of ecstasy born out of meditation; but I am willing to give it a try, and an aged monk leads me out of the vihara into the cloister, where about a hundred men and women, clad in white, are already walking around.

The spectacle resembles a cross between *Agnes of God* and *Dawn of the Dead.* What am I doing in the midst of this zombie movie? But soon, the Wise Old Monk explains. "Stand perfectly still," he says, "breathe deeply ... deeply. Then, set forth ... first your right foot, then your left. Feel the ground beneath your feet, be aware of every speck of dust, every kink and rill in the surface of the stone. With your right foot, think *bud*—. With your left, think — *dho.* Go deliberately, carefully for about twenty-five paces, then stop ... stop completely ... reflect. Then turn. *Bud* —. Right foot, 90° angle, left foot, turn again ... *dho.* Now you are moving in the opposite direction. Slowly ... slowly ... right foot first ... *bud* —. Then left foot ... *dho.* That's all you do."

All? I think to myself. I never knew that mere walking could involve such a complex coordination of thought and movement. I try it. Slowly, I become aware of the texture of the flagstones. Each step seems to stretch out forever ... becoming an adventure in itself.

I walk. I stop. The cloister, aside from being filled with zombies, is lined with life-sized golden Buddhas, and the ashes of the dead, whose faded black-and-white photographs stare back at me from the statues' pedestals. The oddest thing is that, each time I stop to turn, I seem to be face to face with a different Buddha, and each Buddha seems to wear the face of a significant person in my life ... my life outside the walls of the monastery, which is only two days behind me and which already seems remote, untouchable.

My mind seems to detach itself from the body a little: I see myself as a robot, a walking automaton; as my spirit ascends more, I see a pattern emerge; these white-clad meditation students are participants in a cosmic ballet, weaving in and out of each other, always subliminally aware of one another's rhythms, swerving imperceptibly to avoid collisions. It is a beautiful thing. But who is the choreographer, who is the orchestrator?

In the center of the cloister stands a gilded pagoda. I imagine myself at its summit, looking down at the shifting patterns. It is, in microcosm, the dance of the universe: the planets, the moons, the stars, the galaxies. It is stately; it is beautiful; yet

I still experience no catharsis. For I have not yet emptied my mind. I am still burdened by the weight of my own thoughts.

Am I trying too hard?

I groan when I hear that next we will sit in meditation for twenty minutes. (It seems that five minutes will be added for each day of the course, until, by Sunday, we shall be able to go off into a self-induced trance for an hour or more.) I long for release, and yet the very intensity of that longing is preventing it from happening.

Still, the chair helps. I am not in agony.

As I close my eyes and concentrate on the breathing, images of the past distract me. The week before my ordination was, as I've said before, one of exhilaration and turmoil. It haunts me all at once — from lapping up the enthusiasm of the opera fans in San Francisco to my sense of violation at the vandalizing of my home in L.A. — from exciting news about new book deals to betrayals by close friends.

"Forget the past." I hear a voice, gentle, full of concern.

It is the Wise Old Monk. He has been standing in front of me; with my eyes closed, I did not even sense his presence. How did he know that I was being tormented by memories? His apparent ability to read my mind has startled me so much that I obey him without thinking, and for a moment, my mind is emptied of all remembrance.

There is nothing at all.

And then, forming out of the nothing, there is a mountain peak capped with snow. Drenched in sunlight. The sky the brilliant blue of a Ceylon sapphire, the snow so white that it burns like the very sun. I am sure that I know this mountain: it is Kailasa, the legendary dwelling place of the Gods — the Indian Olympus, somewhere in the Himalayas. This isn't just a mental image. I can feel the chill of the mountain wind. It is real.

Slowly, it fades.

Is this the momentary Nirvana that the Guru has been describing? I do not know. And yet, on emerging from my meditative state, I find that I have been weeping.

In the afternoon comes a visit from my mother, the first visit since I bade farewell to my family and was reborn as a symbol of the Sangha. It is strange to have one's own mother prostrate herself, and yet there is a deep pride in her actions; she is acting out a role in an ancient drama that has been played and replayed for twenty-five hundred years.

My mother wants to know whether I need a "luksit", an assistant to fetch and carry, to spend the night in the monastery and walk behind me when I go out with my alms bowl of a morning. I had worried about this; in Thailand, persons of a certain position in society never fetch and carry for themselves, and of course my relatives have been concerned that I won't be able to fend for myself in this alien, harsh environment. But I tell her that the environment isn't particularly harsh, and that I am perhaps more used to fetching and carrying for myself than my relatives. After all, living in the west, one does one's own laundry and dishes. Or at least, machines do. I am sure I can make do without the help.

My mother attempts to pick up and straighten out, but her chauffeur, who once spent time as a novice, warns her that she cannot touch any of the articles used by a monk — the blankets, the towels, and so on. To do so would accidentally involve the monk in an apati. Recoiling in horror, my mother retreats and allows the driver to fold the blankets. I can tell that she's itching to restore the *kuti* to her own well-ordered vision of how a room should look, but now that I have ascended to this higher plane of existence, she can't. It's very strange to see this go-getting woman suddenly stymied by my karmic ascent.

Next, there is the evening chapel; I am getting a little more used to those knee-jarring positions of prostration now, but the evening session is generally a lot longer than the morning, and parts of it are not covered in my romanized Pali manual, but are chanted from a big, fat, somewhat forbidding-looking tome. When Pali is transliterated into Thai, the rules for pronouncing it are quite different from those of Thai, so I flounder around and from time to time am forced into what used to be called, in my days in the Eton College Chapel Choir, the "goldfish trick."

On my way back from the evening chapel, I am faced with a moral dilemma, the first serious one of my monkhood. For, blocking the steps that lead up the outside of the *kuti* to my chamber, there stands a street person — a bum. This is the sort of panhandler one finds aggressively hovering at the entrances of Hyatts and Hiltons in downtown San Francisco, refusing to go away and calling one names until bribed with a dollar bill to bother the next person down the street. The sort of homeless person who accosts one in a parking lot demanding to clean one's car windows even if they are spotless; the kind of person where you turn to whoever you're with and say, "Oh, he'll only spend it on booze."

Such a drunken creature stands in my path now, in the half-dark, his breath stinking of alcohol. "Luang poh," he says, calling me *holy father*, which I still find a little unnerving, "have compassion on me. Please help me to alleviate my karma. I cannot bear my inner torment any longer."

I ask him if there is some moral problem I can help him with, remembering all the times I spoke dismissively to the homeless in my secular days.

He says, "I just need my train fare home so I can take care of my family problems."

I say, "I am a monk. How can you ask me for money? Monks may not even touch money; how could I even lay my hands on some, let alone give it to you?"

It is true. To lay hands on gold and silver (and by extension, on any means of commerce whatsoever) is a violation of not only the 227 rules of monkhood, but even of the mere ten regulations of a novice. There is simply no way I can do as he asks, even though a monk must always be compassionate, even towards those whom he has difficulty feeling compassion for. I am perplexed and lost, and as the bum continues to badger me, I begin to retreat, up the worn stone steps, toward the security and comfort of my airconditioned *kuti*.

All the while cursing my own hypocrisy. After all, Prince Wetsandorn gave away his own *children* to a beggar; why couldn't I find a way of giving the man something? There's always a chance he isn't a drunk really, or that this one donation will be the turning point in his life that causes him to go back to his wife and kids.

Later, I come to learn that there is a small drawer of money somewhere in the *kuti* for such karmic emergencies, and one can, in fact, ask one of the laypersons serving in the temple to take care of mendicants. So I guess this kind of thing happens frequently enough to require a solution.

The little exchange torments me for a while. I have not yet learned one of the great lessons of Buddhism, the art of *ubheka,* of letting go of that which cannot be helped.

In the evening, the Littlest Novice sneaks into my room because he has heard that I have a laptop. "Can you go online?" he asks me excitedly.

"No," I tell him. "Well, I could, but I left my internet access codes back in the outside world. I didn't want email to impinge upon my inward odyssey." He looks at me with cocker spaniel-like eyes, and I realize that this excuse must sound quite pompous to him. He cheers up, however, after I offer him a soda from the huge stockpile of offerings that relatives have been leaving for me all day.

"Do you have any video games?" he persists.

"No," I say. It's for the same reason; I left all those disks behind to avoid being distracted from the great quest.

"How about VCDs?"

"No. Same reason."

"I have a VCD."

"Well, get it, and you can watch it if you like," I tell him, forgetting for a moment that watching a movie might conceivably constitute an *apati*. Oh well, I tell myself, maybe it's a documentary. "What video games do you like, anyway?" I ask him as he sits politely on the floor at my feet in one of those positions of extreme politeness and physical agony that I find so difficult to achieve.

"*Streetfighter II,*" he responds instantly.

I'm a little alarmed at such a love of violence. I wonder whether there's any video game with a more Buddhist flavor.

"You should invent one," he says. "Something about a young novice going around beating up demons and sending them back to the underworld...."

I smile. The saffron robes do not, it seems, change human nature, or boyish high spirits. He tells me he will bring his VCD to try out, but at that moment, eight o'clock arrives and it is time to return to the vihara for evening meditation.

The evening meditation is only for those meditation students who are sleeping over, not the "day students". There's a dormitory where they are housed, and also a nuns' quarter. I don't know where, and I don't ask; there seems no compelling reason to visit those places. In any cases, the meditation students are swarming all over the vihara when I arrive.

I am apprehensive that the Guru will appear; surely, I think, five or six hours' worth of lists of Pali terms is enough for one day. But he does not come down from his *kuti*, and the practice meditation is led by the Wise Old Monk who helped me earlier. All the new monks are there, and all are already seated, lost in their inner explorations. Using the chair, as I did earlier today, I do not experience any visions, but I am at least not suffering physically.

For the walking meditation, we are told that monks may actually ascend to an upper level of the pagoda in the central atrium, where laypersons are not allowed. And so we do so. But the steps are surely made for gods, not men. After some effort, I manage to reach the platform. The pagoda glitters; for though the city's noise pollution is barely audible, Bangkok by night is never dark; the night sky glows with light that has bounced from cloud to cloud, that permeates the very air. There is a breeze up here, a few yards closer to the gods, a godsend after the stifling heat of the day.

Slowly, I walk. I try to cast my mind back to the afternoon, to the vision of Kailasa. The vision haunts me, but it does not return. I walk. The marble flagstones are smooth, warm; all day long they have been sucking up sunlight, storing up heat. I walk. *Bud — dho, bud — dho,* I repeat with each breath.

I still remember the image of the divine mountain, but now that a few hours have passed, I must admit that Kailasa has become confused with the Paramount logo. Trying too hard again, I'm afraid. Yes, I'm acutely, vibrantly aware of the stones, the wind; but no, I am not visited by any visions.

Before I go to bed, I speak on the phone with a friend — it's the first time I've deliberately communicated with the outside world since entering the temple.

My friend, a distant cousin, actually, is a well-known Thai journalist who also reads people's tarot cards, and once performed a goddess ceremony for me in my back yard. So she is not unacquainted with the supernatural.

I tell her of the afternoon's breakthrough ... and the evening's disillusion.

"Don't worry," she tells me. "Seeing a mountain means good news is on the way."

I cling to this idea until dawn.

# The Four Meditating Positions

Traditionally, there are four standard postures in which to perform Buddhist meditation: sitting, walking, standing, and reclining.

You can use the *bud-dho, bud-dho* formula outlined in the previous chapter in order to focus on your breathing, or you can use simple counting, or any number of established mnemonics; you can even use your own. Those who want to divorce their meditation from a strictly "Buddhist" interpretation can either use the pure act of breathing as a focus, words like *in-out, in-out,* or try counting from one to five, or one to ten, in between breathing in and out. *A Clockwork Orange* fans will probably *not* want to use *in-out, in-out,* as it will end up reminding them of, ahem, more worldly subjects.

The sitting meditation traditionally happens in what westerners know as the "lotus" position, that is, cross-legged; you will not go far wrong by emulating the posture of any seated Buddha image. Of course, you might not have such a thing lying around the house.

You can concentrate on any one of three fixed spots, those spots being the tip of the nose, the chest, and the navel.

The standing meditation I found rather hard, as if you close your eyes you have a tendency to start swaying and eventually crash into a wall. You stand serenely with your eyes downcast (or closed) and with your left hand on your abdomen, the right on the left. You concentrate on the ritual formula of your choice.

The walking meditation is a well-known feature of Buddhism, although in my ignorance I was utterly unaware of it until my monkhood. I have described it in detail in the previous chapter, but would add that you need to find a nice, level, straight corridor. A walkway in a park, a cathedral cloister, a quiet stretch of sidewalk, all of these work well; it is best done barefoot, however, in order to extract the full benefit of all the textures of the world that can be sensed through the medium of our humble, overworked feet.

The Guru never mentioned the reclining or sleeping meditation during his seven-day course, but perhaps it was because he didn't want his students to doze off in the middle of the sessions. But I have found it an exceptionally worthwhile method. For me, it doesn't seem to work at the time, but just before waking up, I almost always receive a dream of great vividness that contains the key to some problem that I've been struggling with the previous day.

In the reclining meditation, you lie on your side, "in the posture of a lion," as the manuals put it, basically cushioning the side of your head on an arm; you can see the posture in many famous statues of the Reclining Buddha such as the one at Wat Po in Bangkok. Once in this position, you do the breathing exercise as in the other postures; continue for a set length of time, or better yet, until you become so relaxed that you drift into sleep.

I have found this exercise in focusing one's energy just before retiring for the night to have beneficial effects that last all through the following day.

*Day Three*

# A Momentary Ecstasy

The dawn brings the delivery of a delicious honey-roasted pork from my mother. The plate, piled high, awaits on the lazy susan at breakfast, but of course I am not permitted to show too much enjoyment. Eating with gusto is one of the many things forbidden in the 227 rules of monkhood — along with chewing loudly, taking large mouthfuls, and covering up one's curry with rice so that it appears that one has no curry, and thus tricking one's benefactor into ladling out some more — I kid you not, the latter is actually an official prohibition.

I show no visible gusto, but I do end up with a bit of an upset stomach. Perhaps, I think, meditation will cure it. After all, the Buddha specifically states that walking meditation helps regulate bowel movements.

I spend the hour before morning chapel in my room — I suppose I should call it a cell, as Catholic monks do, but I find it hard to feel any sense of imprisonment when the room has both air conditioning and a private bathroom. There is a beautiful chair in the room, inlaid with mother-of-pearl and doubtless worth a hundred thousand baht. Although the room itself is spartan in its furnishings, each simple object is an exquisite work of art. A lot of love and thought has been devoted to this room.

In the chair, alone, without two hundred others meditating around me, I try once more to empty my mind. I think it is starting to work ... no Mount Kailasa, no flashes, but a pervasive calm.

Morning chapel is an ordeal, still. I wonder why "arthritis" is not among the list of diseases they interrogate you about in the ceremonial inquisition before you become a monk. After all, they ask you if you're a leper. Today, we know that leprosy is only infectious amongst a tiny percentage of the genetically predisposed. They also ask if you're a cripple. That would never fly in politically correct America. Asking whether you're human or not — well, that I can understand. You never know what kind of demoniacal being might want to seek refuge in a monastery.

Had they asked me, in Pali, about arthritis, I could have answered with a snappy *"ama bhante"* and ended up with a medical release from monkhood. But no.

So here I am, with my romanized manual before me, last monk on the far right in the back, chanting up a storm.  The chanting begins with standard phrases about Buddha, Dhamma, and Sangha, but then enters unfamiliar territory with long sections chanted half in Thai and half in Pali.  The Thai is supposed to be the translation of the Pali, so it is hard to understand why a single Pali word can be followed by an entire sentence of Thai.  Presumably it because Pali is one of those languages in which a little utterance can mean a lot — ancient languages all seem to share that characteristic.  I remember this from struggling through Ovid in school.

The odd thing is, much of the Pali chanting bears a certain similarity to Latin.  (Sanskrit, I understand from a brief look at a few textbooks, is somewhat more like Greek.)  Pali has the rhythms of Latin, with the verbs chiming in at the end, with the cases, persons, numbers, and tenses lined up in neat little rows with their endings all matching; it's almost like Latin with an Indian accent.

The chanting is addictive, hypnotic even.  But I notice that attendance at morning chapel doesn't seem to be that strictly enforced.  Monks wander in and out, and seem automatically to glide into their proper place.  Behind the monks, the novices are supposed to sit, but only one has shown up, and another is drifting in.

It's not really polite to stare at the spectacle around me, but I can't help myself.  I force myself to resume chanting.

Suddenly, a high-pitched, boyish treble voice joins in the chanting. Whoever it is knows the words perfectly, chants with utter confidence, his voice soaring above the others, adding a bell-like resonance to the masculine bass that roils about the chapel. I glance behind my shoulder and see that the Littlest Novice has finally shown up — the one who wanted to create a video game and monks battling demons with weird martial arts.

Now, inside this sacred place, he is a completely different boy. The chant flows from his lips as from the lips of an angel. He is transported. This place does change people. The street urchin has become divine.

As I prostrate myself, later, before the Guru in readiness for the morning meditation class, I thank him for teaching me the wherewithal to see the vision of Mount Kailasa.

"Ah," he says, nodding knowingly. "That vision was a *nimit.*"

What he means by that is that I did not see the true Mount Kailasa, but an image manufactured in the depths of my unconscious mind. He tells me that *nimits* can be both beautiful and dangerous, and if I find myself distracted by one, I must act as though it isn't there. He sends me back to my chair, and proceeds to address the subject of death.

Death, along with love, is what human beings are most preoccupied with.

What is death? This is what the Guru chooses to discourse on, at length, before the daily meditation

begins.   We learn that the flesh is inherently
degenerate, that our body is a graveyard for the
corpses of pigs and chickens.   We listen to an
enumeration of the thirty-two unpleasant parts of
the body, spending as much time on excrement and
mucus as on prettier organs such as skin and hair.

We learn that death is the very definition of life,
for what is a living thing but a piece of earth that
has somehow fended off death for a few brief
moments of existence?   Well, this is all very
depressing, and I understand why some people
think Buddhism is overly pessimistic: nothing
exists, we're all going to die, the best thing we can
hope for is go out like a candle instead of being
endlessly reborn and suffering ... a few thousand
lifetimes can really get on one's nerves.   So, when
we reenter the inner world to begin the morning's
meditation, I am not a happy camper.

And yet ... today's journey into the unconscious
is a roller coaster ride.   Yesterday it was all effort,
and my reward was a momentary glimpse of the
abode of the gods; today, I slide right in, my mind
draining instantly, like a colander of fresh spaghetti.

First, in the darkness, there is a face.   I see the
face dimly at first.   It's dark, but its outlines radiate
a certain energy.   There's the faintest hint of a
moustache, and great brooding eyes.   The chair I'm
sitting in faces the left side of the great golden
Buddha that dominates the vihara; on either side,
there are huge statues of *arahants*, their gaze
permanently fixed in adoration of the great master.

The face in my mind's eye seems to match the faces of these *arahants*, faces I have never seen because the statues have their backs to me, because they are gazing upward at the Lord Buddha. The face's features are somewhat Indian, I think to myself, wavering in the shadows. Is this an ancient sage, or is it again a *nimit,* a figment of my imagination? I sink deeper into the meditative trance. I see pagodas shifting in the mist. I see stone ruins, minarets, walls covered with bas-reliefs. In niches and nooks, tiny stone devas are frozen in elaborate dance gestures.

A kind of warmth steals over me. An inner warmth, different from the heat that pervades the vihara, intermittently alleviated by a turning electric fan. This warmth has a color to it as well, a deep red, and begins with a glow at the tips of my fingers and toes, works its way up the limbs, seems to center itself on a spot somewhere in the middle of my forehead. This must be what mystics call the Third Eye, what others refer to as the pineal gland. This is the spot where Hindus traditionally place those caste marks that have caused some in the west jeeringly to refer to them as dotheads. This dot is positively glowing, radiating energy.

And growing, too. The dot becomes a circle. It shifts from red to white, from lukewarm to incandescent. I can barely keep my eyes closed, there's so much light. And then, within the light, I begin to make out the silhouette of some ancient personage. It is someone sacred. I am sure of it. I am certain that if I can let go just a little bit more, I will even hear this personage speak. It is not the Buddha himself — I do not think so — though the apparition stands serenely, his hair spiraling upward as though aflame, one hand reaching out, palm forward, as if to bless, to touch —

And then there is a touch. On my shoulder.

Startled, I open my eyes. It is the Guru, who has left his preaching chair and has been wandering around the vihara, looking over his charges. "Your posture," he says mildly. "A little straighter. That's it, that's it."

Was it the Guru that I sensed, hovering in the circle of light within my inner world? He is standing exactly where the ancient personage seemed to appear in my vision. Is this some kind of cosmic joke, or did I somehow have a brief encounter with the Guru's spiritual essence?

All I know is that I have been jolted out of the meditative state. I struggle to suppress a certain irritation. After all, I was about to be addressed by some ancient sage, only to find myself being curtly spoken to by an earthly guru. Clearly, however, this is another lesson in humility.

Later, it is lunchtime, and a little huckster stand outside the vihara does a brisk business in the Guru's self-help books as I, the Intellectual, and the other new monks enjoy a simple but abundant meal of honey-roasted pork, duck, satays, Chinese pasta, and exotic fruits. Well, they are exotic to me, at least. You can't find a decent mango in America.

After we eat, all the monks chant a prayer of extraordinary beauty — the *yatha varivaha*. It is only later that I realize just how beautiful it is; at the moment it is mere nonsense syllables, and it seems that even to many of the new monks, they have little meaning save for the hypnotic quality of the sounds themselves.

But later I am to learn the meaning of this blessing, chanted by monks, somewhere, every single day in Thailand in every single place where monks are being served by laypersons, a blessing so commonplace that children can repeat it word for word like parrots, a blessing whose translation few people know.

> *As the rivers full of water*
> *flow into the great ocean,*
> *so let the merit you have made*
> *benefit the dead;*
> *may what you have wished*
> *come quickly to pass,*
> *may your wishes grow to fulfillment*
> *as the moon that waxes on the fifteenth night,*
> *as the jewel that grants desires.*

The monks chant enthusiastically, and I, knowing neither the words not their meaning, feel ever an outsider, ever an alien.

But then, that afternoon, there comes the payoff. The Guru has added another five minutes to the clock — bringing the total to thirty minutes of concentrated breathing — a longer span than I have ever imagined I could do. But this time, the visions come immediately. The circles of light, the *arahants* gazing on their Lord in eternal adoration, whirling about, circles within circles … all these images drift through my mind with renewed clarity. The irregular movement of the electric fan, the beading and coalescing of drops of sweat on my brow, the sighs of an elderly gentleman as he wheezes through the breathing exercises … yes, I have become aware of all these things. And then, without warning, I push through to another level. The circles of light spin ever faster, and then, all at once, there are waves of light, breaking across my consciousness, torrents and tides of blinding whiteness. And fireworks! Coruscating, scintillant rainbow rivers spiral and twist and whirl.

I am lost in wonderment, lost in an ecstasy that far exceeds that of any hallucinogenic experiment I may or may not have undertaken in the 60s (which if I did, I surely can't remember now!) So this is what it's all about — this is the psychedelic symphony of light described by such mystics as Coleridge and Blake.

Abruptly, the little beep-beep-beep sounds, signaling the end of the thirty minutes.

"Come out of the meditation slowly," the Guru's voice cautions over the vihara's speaker system.

Slowly, slowly, the vision subsides.

The Guru warns us not to be seduced by the beauty of visions. They are *nimits,* he tells us ... sometimes they can mislead ... entrap.

And yet, I know I am on the verge of something big.

The evening is a bit of a party night. My nephew, a music student at Mahidol University, drops by; my parents pop in for a visit; and as the sun sets, the Seer, surrounded by a small congregation of my relatives, decides to tell us inspiring stories from the life of the Buddha; his memory is limitless, his narrative technique worthy of an ancient bard, singing tales at the dinner table of a Viking chieftain or a Mycenaean King.

One question has been bothering me since I stumbled across it in my English language manual, the one that gives all the translations of these quaint Pali texts. "Why, Lord Seer," I ask him, "am I agreeing that I can only bathe every fifteen days?"

My mother says, "Oh, nonsense. How could the Buddhist texts possibly tell one to refrain from bathing? The ancient Buddhists weren't dirty."

The Seer laughs. "Well, yes, there is such a prohibition," he tells us, "and it came about because, one day, the Buddha was preaching in a remote place, in which there was only one small stream available for bathing. The members of the nobility who had come to hear the sermon couldn't get back to their city before the gates closed, and the stream was clogged with the disciples of the Lord

Buddha. Out of consideration for the supplicants, the Buddha created that rule ... but you see, it only applies in that one location, in that particular circumstance."

It seems, then, that the monastic regulations are a sort of mishmash of precedent and custom. Rather like the English common law, they have grown over time and developed into a rather complex, even hairsplitting code.

At eight o'clock comes the special late-night meditation in the vihara. And now, something *really* weird happens to me.

I try to repeat the success of the afternoon. At first it seems easy enough. I slip quickly into the state I was in just before the big fireworks and the tides of light. It's about ten minutes or so in, I guess.

Then yes — again — that blinding incandescent light —

And then — complete emptiness.

I know nothing until I hear the beeping, telling us that it is time to come slowly forth from the inner world.

I know I was not asleep. I *know* this. After all, I have woken up several thousand times in my life, and know what it is to have just slept. This was not like that. This was not a state of sleep. It was *nothing*. Nothing at all.

Was this, in fact, at last, the momentary Nirvana so rapturously described by the Guru the previous day? If so ... why can't I remember anything at all?

It's like that poem by Keats. You know, the one where the knight meets a gorgeous elfin lady who takes him to her grotto and seduces him until —

*And I awoke, and found me here,*
*On the cold hill's side.*

Is that one of the attributes of the state of ultimate nothingness — that the nothingness is so absolute that nothing can remain even in the remembrance of it?

I do not know.

I resolve to try a fresh tactic tonight. In the Guru's instruction manual, of which I have an English-language copy, there are four postures of meditation: sitting, standing, walking, and ... sleeping. We have not yet tried the sleeping style. It doesn't look like the Guru is going to cover the sleeping meditation in this seven-day course.

And yet, there comes a time in any journey when one must leave one's guide behind and take a few tentative steps alone.

Tonight, I decide, I'm going to try it for myself.

# Such a Piti: Ecstasy Defined

What is ecstasy?  Well, here comes another of those infamous lists that Buddhism has bequeathed to us.  In what follows, I am more or less re-telling what the Guru described to us in his lecture.

It is said that meditation can give rise to certain ecstatic states of mind that are known as *piti*. Naturally, these states have not only been catalogued, but have difficult Pali names.  One would expect no less of Buddhism, which, for a philosophy whose basic revelation is that nothing exists, seems to spend a great deal of time defining those very things that it says do not exist.

It is said that these different forms of *piti* evince themselves when the meditator has started to approach the state of *samadhi* or one-pointedness.

*Khuddaka-piti* is a sort of "little ecstasy." Your hair stands on end, perhaps, or a tear rolls down your cheek. *Khanika-piti,* a momentary ecstasy, is sort of like flashes or spasms, or weird little creepy-crawlies wandering around on your face. *Okkantika-piti,* an "intermittent" ecstasy, is more wavelike. Tides of joy, waves beating against the shores of the soul. *Ubbenka-piti* is defined as a more dramatic sort of piti, in which one feels buoyant, one's soul seems to fly around the place — it is rumored that even physical levitation can occur in this state, though I'll be honest, I didn't see anything that might defy the laws of physics in the vihara.

The Guru has spent some time discussing levitation, and the legends of various people who, in the throes of this particular piti, have experienced astral projection, psychokinesis, and teleportation. Well, all right, in my fictional works, I write about such things all the time, but I like to think of myself as rather more firmly rooted in the real world, and I must confess that I find it a little disturbing that the *feeling* of rising into the air and the physical act of defying gravity are being discussed in the same sentence. But, for now, we will let that pass.

The final ecstasy is called *pharana-piti,* and is characterized by a pervasive joy, a glow from within. According to the Guru's textbook, this is a piti that takes over one's whole being, filling it with a quiet joy.

I believe that I may have felt this last *piti* during the missing minutes of meditation described in the previous chapter. If so, I grasp at the remembrance now as one might grasp the empty air.

Like the notorious eighteen-minute gap in the Nixon Watergate tapes, those missing moments are probably playing forever in some closed loop, some recursive dimension. Like the inside of a black hole.

In retrospect, that's probably exactly where I was.

*Day Four*

# The Begging Bowl

My attempts at sleep meditation do not seem to have borne fruit. I sleep fitfully. Partially it is nervousness; in the morning I am to step out of the monastery alone for the first time. One of the most inviolable precepts of monkhood is that one may not work for, earn, or in any way strive to attain personal comfort. Eating is a particularly complex issue. The rule is that one must not take that which is not freely given, and in the case of food this generally means walking around in the morning with a begging-bowl.

For the first three days of monkhood, one is sequestered within the monastery walls, and isn't allowed to go out foraging in the streets. Now, you might think that this has to do with a sort of ritual immersion in spirituality … the idea that you need to become wholly and utterly sanctified before setting foot beyond the gate. After all, three is a magic number in all cultures. For example, from Neolithic mother-goddess cults all the way to Christianity, any divine being wishing to come back from the dead is expected to grant the living the courtesy of staying down under for three days. No self-respecting being expects to be resurrected overnight. You'd think that the three-day quarantine is all about that, but it's not. Like many other Buddhist customs, it's purely practical.

Three days is the average time it takes for a monk to learn how to walk around without his robes falling off.

On the fourth morning of monkhood, I learn that I am somewhat below average in this respect. My morning struggle with the robes has yet to yield an elegant result. Nevertheless, after about half an hour, I emerge from my room with the robes more-or-less attached and with the little tail that one uses to twist and tighten it sticking firmly out from under my left armpit. I'm sure Sigmund Freud would have seen some phallic imagery there, but, quickly remembering that I am supposed to be beyond such metaphors, I quickly dismiss them from my mind. Gathering up my bowl, I march proudly out to face the secular cosmos.

I don't get very far. Only two steps from my room, I run into the Maha, who gazes at my attire in horror.

"Oh dear, oh dear," he says, "you're wearing your robe all wrong."

"No, I'm not," I insist. After all, I *have* followed the instructions pretty faithfully. And usually there's a forewarning before the robes drop off — a twitching of the fabric somewhere, a shifting in the folds. "Don't worry, I think I can manage a ten minute walk without an embarrassing incident."

"Well, you seem to have figured it out all right," says the Maha, "but you see, when you go outside the temple, you have to wear the robes in a different style."

Now I suddenly recall one of those 227 monastic precepts — it's about going completely covered when a monk goes among laypersons. I had thought that I *was* completely covered, but in fact, inside the temple, one goes about with one's right shoulder exposed.

Presumably, it wouldn't do to inflame any passing laywomen to see that little piece of shoulder, and so yes, there's a completely different way of wearing your robes when you set foot outside the gates. And that, as the dawn begins to break over the temple's gilded gables, is what I must now proceed to learn — and fast, because after all, the hordes of well-wishers with their offerings of food are not going to hang around forever.

They've got skytrains to catch.

A few days ago I already gave one description of how to wear those robes; a second, contradictory description would probably not be very useful. So, suffice it to say that, beginning with finding the little square of cloth that aligns with the back of one's neck, there's a completely new system of twirling and wrapping to be learned, and the end result is that the monk, with his begging bowl *inside* the robes and accessible only by manipulating a little flap, is totally rolled up inside that rectangle of saffron, much like a piece of ravioli, or rather, I should say, a wonton.

I had thought that the previous style of monkly couture was a little stifling, but this is positively suffocating at first. However, the mode of dress lends itself to those delicate, deliberate steps that one always sees monks taking as they move slowly down the alleys in the dawn. Now I understand why; the full-wrap technique winds you up so tightly that it is impossible to be anything *but* delicate and deliberate in one's movements.

Oh yes, the hands. The left hand, supporting the bowl so that it doesn't go bouncing on the pavement, is completely concealed. Well, left hands, in Asian cultures, are pretty unseemly anyway; one knows what they are traditionally used for. But the right hand, too, is hidden in this style of dress. Only by wriggling its way through a tightly wound roll of fabric can the hand create a little slit for itself and emerge to open the lid of the alms bowl or manipulate small objects.

It is with a certain measure of self-consciousness that I finally manage to make my way down the steps of the *kuti*. The Maha, who in addition to showing me the ropes, performs the function of a sort of babysitter, leads the way. I do not wear my sandals. This is a very strict monastic order — some do, in fact, allow monks to wear sandals for this ritual — but we must, like the Lord Buddha himself, go completely barefoot into the world, heedless of the thorns, snakes, bugs, mud, and gravel that might assault our delicate, city-bred soles.

The back door of the temple leads to a parking lot, and then to a little alley bordered by noodle stands, before reaching the main road. It is morning, and the Maha walks much faster than I do, so I find myself alone in the alley. This is it, I tell myself. This is the "going-forth", as the English-language monkhood manual so grandly calls it, a descent from Parnassus into the seamy secular cosmos.

There is a moment of panic, but all at once, the technique of the walking meditation takes over. I take one step at a time. Slowly, breathing deeply, trying to become aware of each minuscule sensation. One step, then another.

Why is it that we are commanded to go barefoot into the world? To show our humility, no doubt, our vulnerability; to be a living metaphor of the frailty that is flesh.

These sound like very negative reasons, but there is another, more positive one. The skin is a living, breathing organ, the organ of the human body that has the largest area, the greatest sensitivity to the outside world. And the earth beneath our feet is the earth that gave us birth, our mother, the earth that will receive us once our struggle against entropy has ended. Children may run barefoot in the grass, but as adults we shield ourselves from the earth; the act of putting on shoes is an act of subversion, of resistance to reality.

Shoes? Why, in Los Angeles, one doesn't even walk at all. Not only are one's feet shielded from the earth, but even one's shoes; I for one use the drive-through for my ATM, my diet Pepsi, and my car wash.

Not for a long time have I felt against my feet the sharpness of a cobblestone, squeezed moisture from the moss in the cracks of concrete. Not for a long time have I swerved to sidestep the squish of excrement between bare toes or the crunch of a dying cockroach.

I suddenly grasp that these homely sensations, these textures of reality, forgotten since God knows when, are a severed link in the chain of being.

The journey down the alley, which only takes a minute, is in itself a miniature voyage of discovery.

Or rediscovery.

Once I emerge from the alley, I see the Maha across the street; he has gone to the newsstand to fetch the Seer's daily newspaper. I hug the alms bowl to my chest and twirl the tail of my robe in order to hitch it a little higher so that it won't drag on the pavement. Then, taking my life in my hands as all Bangkokian pedestrians do, I cross the street.

The other side of the street consists mostly of shophouses: pharmacies, electrical appliance stores, and newsstands with living quarters in their upper storeys. In front of one of the ubiquitous Chinese pharmacies, a wooden table has been set out, and there are trays of food: little plastic bags of curry and soup, and cups of boiled rice. There is a bit of a cottage industry as the faithful line up to buy food which they will in turn offer to the monks.

My first benefactor is a man I've seen, all in white, at the meditation class; I've seen him sitting not far from me, lost in thought. I wonder if he even recognizes me. I am, after all, not a person anymore, but a metaphor, and a pathway for his own karmic journey. Gingerly, I lift the lid of the bowl. He empties a cup of rice into it, and puts in a bag of curry. My eyes remain downcast, as is seemly. I do not proffer thanks; that too is improper in this ritual. It is the strangest thing to me that I cannot show him this common courtesy, but it would diminish the karmic value of his gift to me.

I see the Maha in a dark alley nearby. I follow. Suddenly, I am in a marketplace, hidden from the street by the façades of the shophouses. It is so early that many of the stalls are still untended. Still, there are people everywhere. Dawn is the time to make merit before picking up the groceries for the kitchen back home. This isn't a shiny American-style supermarket, where the odors of fresh food are

carefully masked by layers of Saran wrap.   Here,
every kind of scent assaults one, from the noxious
fumes of leaking petrol to the fragrance of jasmine,
of rose petals.

A bleary-eyed woman turns chicken drumsticks
on a grill.   Another arranges flower garlands on
rattan trays.  The market is dingy; the dawn has not
penetrated, and here and there a naked bulb sheds
harsh light over a pile of durian or an old man
blending milk and coffee in a glass urn.  The concrete
paving is moist and warm; grit works itself between
my toes.  There are monks here, each one moving in
a sort of bubble of solitude, for though shopping in
Bangkok is very much a contact sport, the throng
parts each time a monk moves through.

As I follow the Maha, his shaven head bobbing
up and down in the distance, I too sense the parting
of the crowd; I am like a mini-Moses breasting the
Red Sea.  The yellow robe really does make me
something other than myself.  There is an unseen
radiance that envelops me.

When I have given food to monks in the past, I
have often been distracted by the thought that hey,
maybe they won't even eat it, or perhaps they're not
even going to like it, or some monasteries are so
bloated with offerings the leftovers must surely end
up in the garbage.   But as I accept the people's
offerings, their piety overwhelms my skepticism.  I
am of course precisely repeating the footsteps of the
earliest Buddhist monks. I feel the weight of history;
I feel like a tiny pattern within an immense and

ever-turning mandala; and this sense of belonging somehow subsumes my doubt.

Well, back the *kuti,* it occurs to me that when the bags of food arrive at the breakfast table, they're not the same bags that were offered to me in the marketplace. In fact, the food seems a lot more to my liking now than it did then. In fact, those little muffins on the tray by my place at the table ... well, I don't remember receiving those at all. They are a sort of Chinese variant of those blueberry muffins that are such a fixture of breakfast in American greasy spoons.

I am not, of course, allowed to evince any kind of preference for one kind of food over another; but I suspect that there's been some Machiavellian maneuvering in the kitchens of the *kuti,* and that someone has conspired to mix up the bags so that this Thai monk who isn't quite Thai can be allowed to eat some farang food that isn't quite farang.

Having successfully avoided several large piles of dog turds during my perambulation of the marketplace, I run into an extremely large pile during the Guru's morning lecture on meditation. He chooses to use shit as a metaphor for karma. Once again, I am impressed with the ubiquity of bodily functions in Buddhist philosophy. The King James Bible seldom mentions excrement; I can think of only one instance offhand, and that's in the Old Testament.

The Guru tells us a parable. In ancient times, he says, in India, naturally, the land of parables, two indigents are walking down the street, each carrying an empty basket. They see an enormous pile of dried excrement in the road. "We can sell this as fertilizer," they tell each other, and they eagerly fill their baskets, place them on their heads, and go off through the forest, on the road to the nearest town.

They come across a pile of dried wood. One of them, the cleverer of the two, presumably says, "Well, let's trade in our shit for this dried wood, which will fetch a much higher price in the town."

His friend says, "I've been carrying this shit for so long; I think I'll wait until something better shows up."

They wander through the forest some more, and they stumble on an abandoned cart filled with bolts of expensive silk. Well, you can see where the story is leading. From silk to silver to gold to piles of diamonds, the clever one keeps upgrading his basket, while the other one, faithfully plodding along, says, "I've been carrying this shit for so long, I think I'll wait just a bit more."

They reach the city at last, and the clever man turns in his precious cargo for a huge fortune and lives happily ever after. His stupid friend doesn't really mind; he's not the jealous type; he's not a bad person, you see, and he is perfectly happy to trade in the basket of dried excrement that he's been carrying on his head for so very long. But just as he reaches the fertilizer shop, it begins to rain....

With this repulsive image fresh in our minds, the Guru then says, "Now, students, I'm going to add another five minutes to the clock ... and I want you all to empty your minds and meditate for thirty-five minutes."

Lunch today features one of the most famous chocolate cakes in Bangkok, made by the hand of M.R. Malinee, a friend of my mother's and creator of this well-known recipe. My mother and sister have surveyed the various offerings in the *kuti,* and have decided that the roast duck down the alley is probably a better deal. They vanish for a while, leaving me alone with the Seer and the chocolate cake.

The Seer looks at me and says, "You shouldn't go back to America yet. Your chart shows a cloud that extends over your life all the way until at least February 2002. Becoming a monk has mitigated what could have happened — it was a sort of surgical solution to your inner turmoil. But you're in danger until at least October, and the shadow will not utterly pass until February."

"But I do have commitments," I tell him. "Books to write and whatnot."

"Other factors will intervene," he says. "You will be fine here."

I do not know how clearly he sees into my heart. I do not entirely understand why, only two weeks ago, a voice whispered in my ear that I must begin this inward journey. I am troubled by things left undone, by my condo in Los Angeles left in disarray, even by the fact that — now that I think of it — I didn't turn on the dishwasher before I left California. And yes, the dishwasher thing has been gnawing at me from time to time.

"Let it go," says the Seer. "You can buy more dishes."

The Seer has endowed an upcountry temple that specializes in the teaching of novices, many of them poor kids who would not otherwise have a chance to go to a decent school. He suggests to me that perhaps, if I stay at the monastery, I could be placed in charge of the entire *kuti,* and he could spend more time at the rural wat, where, I suspect, his real heart lies, for he was born and raised in Thailand's deep south.

The idea of being placed in charge of an entire division of a monastery when I have in fact only been here for a few days is strange to me. On the other hand, the Seer seems to suggest it in all seriousness, and I realize that even in a few days, I have become accepted here, eccentricities and all; being a monk is not, despite the shaved heads and identical robes, about conforming. Every monk here is on a unique journey, and every journey is equally deserving of respect.

I decide that I will, next time I get near the internet, transmit this to Sharon and Tomm; perhaps they will have another perspective on it all.

It is now time for the afternoon session of the meditation workshop, and *piti* is the word of the day.

My companion-in-suffering, the Intellectual, tells me he hasn't managed to achieve any kind of *piti* whatsoever. He has tried and tried. The aches and pains of an aging body, forced to hold weird positions for long periods, have militated against *piti*. I ask him if he's tried the chair thing. I know I couldn't have done it without a chair.

He whispers in my ear, "Seriously, though, I think there's another reason why it's never worked out. You see ... I don't entirely ... *believe.*"

But I don't entirely believe either ... at least, I don't *think* I do. But *piti* has still descended on my doubting mind. Before I can argue this point, though, he says, "I'm too angry. That's it, I'm just too irritated at all the superstition."

I believe that the Intellectual is experiencing some disillusionment. It's because of what I mentioned briefly in the chapter defining *piti*. The fact that levitation in the imagination was bandied about in the same breath as levitation in actuality. The Intellectual doesn't buy this, and it colors his perception of the entire process.

"You know," I say, "maybe it's better *not* to think about these things too much. We should take from this teaching what we are able to accept, and let the rest go."

"I know," he says. "But it's a bit of a leap to go from penetrating psychological insight to — fables and hearsay about people flitting through the air like in low-budget Indian epics."

There may be many doubters, but the Intellectual is the only one with the courage to express doubt openly. His honesty touches me.

We continue to listen to the discourse on *piti,* but I am too distracted to enter a deep state of meditation; I am haunted by images of my home in Los Angeles, and by the Seer's obscure predictions of a shadowed future.

After the evening chapel, I have a surprise visit from my Uncle Mai, his friend, and my cousin, and I show them around my quarters — I feel like a little boy again, you know, when friends come over and your mother says, "Now, why don't you show Little Jethro your room?" They prostrate themselves and present me with several dozen containers of fruit juice — the best quality — as well as the Oriental Hotel's prized cookies. Then they proceed to admire the furnishings — the air conditioning with its remote control, the private bathroom that even has its own urinal despite the fact that it is against the 227 rules for monks to pee standing up.

After they leave, my nephew, Pup, comes by; he's been studying for a test at Mahidol, and he has his homework with him; he asks me a few questions about four-part harmony.

The Littlest Novice shows up. He has the VCD he told me he wanted to watch on my computer. To my amazement, it is a pirated edition of the *Spice Girls* movie. Heavens! Is this too lewd for a young novice to watch, I wonder? I decide to let the kid be a kid, and I put it on while Pup babysits (or is it the novice who is babysitting my nephew?) and then I am summoned for the evening meditation.

That's where I have my miraculous experience of the day. It is during walking meditation, and it has started to drizzle. All the monks and supplicants have scurried to take cover under the roof of the cloister or inside the vihara. But for some reason I don't notice this at first, so concerned am I with the act of putting one foot in front of the other.

The wind begins to blow. It's a warm, moist wind; in the tropics, in the midst of the rainy season, the wind that presages rain is not a hurtful wind. It plays with the hem of these robes, but I walk on. It billows a little, but I am only dimly aware of it at first.

The rain comes. A little at a time. I become conscious of each individual raindrop as it glances off my skin. I breathe, I walk, I stop, I turn. The marble pavement becomes slick, as though stone itself were sweating. The rain falls harder now, and as it pelts down I feel what I have rarely felt in my adult life — I feel enveloped in, caressed by the forces of nature. Nothing can harm me. The rain spins about me a silken cocoon of being, of immediacy. This is another *piti:* not an experience of inner reality, but a more profound embrace of the external world. There is an aspect of Buddhism that emphasizes withdrawal and detachment, but tonight I am feeling the opposite; I am the plaything of the earth and sky, a figment of the world's imagination.

Though nature is vast and I am small and helpless, I feel nurtured; I feel loved.

Well, after that, my sitting meditation is something of an anticlimax. And when I ask my friend, the Intellectual, whether he has finally achieved any *piti,* he says to me, "I appear to have snoozed off."

"Don't worry," I say to him. "It's only, what, the third day of the meditation class; we have four more to go."

He smiles ruefully. "That's true," he says. "Well, maybe my karma just isn't up to it. Or maybe it will be all the sweeter for coming at the eleventh hour."

# Four Recollections

Monks must ever be mindful of four "recollections".

Actually if you look this up online you'll find that there are many lists of recollections, three, four, five or more, but at Wat Somanas I was told of four.

Naturally, each of the four was further subdivided because complex taxonomy seems to be an obsession in all Indian philosophies; I rather doubt that the Buddha himself had prepared so many lists and schemes.

The ones we're talking about now, since meditation was the Abbot's big "thing", are "foundations of mindfulness" — four broad categories of meditational objects that can help bring one to a state of mindfulness.

A real exegesis of this subject would take up the whole book but I just want to give a flavor of it.

So first ... *Mindfulness of the Body.* This is a great meditative exercise for someone like me because I write horror novels, and I'm particularly drawn to "subset 6" of this, known as the cemetery meditation.

What you do is imagine a corpse, slowly rotting, and, as in all these enumerations, there are listed steps to help you in visualization (I didn't write this down at the time, but the internet has provided me with the following stages of decomposition)

*the festering body (a few days old)*
*the corpse being devoured by birds, beasts and worms*
*a skeleton held together by tendons, with some flesh and blood remaining*
*a skeleton held together by tendons, fleshless, smeared with blood*
*a skeleton held together by tendons, fleshless and bloodless*
*loose bones scattered about*
*bones bleached white by the sun*
*bones a year old lying piled in a heap*
*rotted bones crumbling to dust ...*

This is sort of like virtual time-lapse photography. Scenes of, say, a vampire crumbling to dust are a common feature of my childhood fantasies, fed as they are on Hammer's horror films and Christopher Lee.

So if the intent of this exercise is to evoke horror, it didn't quite work with me.

One also has to meditate on how disgusting the human body is, this old sack of meat and bones, and the texts have cleverly listed thirty-two areas on which to focus, viz. *"hair of the head, hair of the body, nails, teeth, skin, flesh, sinews, bones, marrow, kidneys, heart, liver, membranes, spleen, lungs, bowels, intestines, gorge, dung, bile, phlegm, pus, blood, sweat, fat, tears, grease, snot, spittle, oil-of-the-joints, urine ..."*

I did not memorize this either, but pulled the list from the web.

By the time one has gone through all that, one ought to be quite mortified by all this mortification, so it's time to elevate the meditative objects and enter higher recollections.

So, after the body come the emotions, *vedana.* These, too, are classified. Thirdly, we have the mind itself ... the states of consciousness ... and finally, *dhammas* ... mind objects which are sort of abstractions made concrete by our ability to visualize them ... finally leading, through an evolutionary process of contemplation, to the Four Noble Truths.

But we shall speak of those in another chapter.

*Day Five*

# Lucid Dreaming

The previous night, I have been attempting, once more, this reclining meditation. Nothing seems to happen, although I do drift off into a profound sleep. But, just before dawn, I have an astonishingly vivid dream.

I see a person I've never seen in one of my dreams before. He's the ringleader of the kids who vandalized my house in Los Angeles, several months before my coming to Bangkok to be a monk. This is someone who was highly successful in triggering my martyrdom instinct — and who, until I learned what had been happening behind my back, was one of my most trusted people. I will call him simply the Kid; there isn't another in this story.

We're standing in a museum, carrying a Persian rug between us. And the Kid is complaining about something or other — about how Africa isn't in the exhibition, I think. So the museum guard says to us, well, there's an Egyptian exhibition in the next building; it's been there for a year and is set to remain for a total of two; and we decide to check it out, still carrying the rug. Though I have to remind the Kid that Egypt is, in fact, in Africa; he doesn't seem to have learned that in school.

I enter the museum; the Kid stands in the anteroom, in front of the revolving door, still holding the rug. I go through, look in the gift shop for more rugs; I decide they're too expensive. I don't remember actually looking at the exhibits; all I know is that the Kid never enters, and when I start to leave, he is gone, and instead there are two lines of graffiti on the wall, written in marker, already fading … medium fine point marker, bright red, the color of blood.

Outside, the scenery has abruptly changed. I am in the ruins of an ancient temple. Gray, decaying stone … it's beautiful, like Ayuthaya used to be in my childhood, before easy-access highways and wandering tourists. There are stupas, gorgeous statues of stone and stucco; the sky is a ruddy twilight. I am walking through the grounds, slowly, in a meditative state … more so than I have achieved during real life walking meditation.

Suddenly, a huge gray pagoda rears up in the sunrise. I spot two kids half-way, on a ledge, graffitiing with spray cans. I am furious. I run up the steps, I scream at them: "Don't you realize this place is unimaginably ancient, it was lifted stone by stone from an archaeological site and brought here to be shared by all the world?  Thousands of years of history and you're ruining it ... there's a place for what you're doing, but not here!"

Chastened, they slink away.

Startled, I awaken.

I'm sure it is almost dawn, but I get up and look, in the dark, at the clock; it seems to say that it's eleven at night.  I try to get back to sleep.  Dogs are barking ... as they do in movies when a ghost or spirit passes.  My whole body is tingling ... as though I have recently been possessed, and the alien presence's breath is still exuding from me.  I can't or won't find the light switch; I am groping about in a strange half-dark.  This *Twilight Zone*-like weirdness persists for a very long time; I lie down, trying to return to sleep, vaguely aware that I've had a very powerful dream that is trying to teach me important lessons about my past, my future.

I close my eyes for a moment, and then —

Jumping out of bed, I find that it's after six!  I have to run out with my begging bowl!  Seizing my bowl and robe, I run out of the door just in time for a helpful monk to put it on for me.

It has just been raining, and I tread along the wet street, absorbing more unfamiliar sensations — the slick cobblestones, the grit, the agglutinating particles of earth.  It is a beautiful experience sharing the love and generosity of people I have never met or known.  I wish I could walk among them all the time.  I am at the same time a stranger to these people, and the most familiar icon in their perception of the world.

It is breakfast now, and they have decided that the four of five pieces of the Khunying's famed chocolate should be offered to me all once. I decide to take the entire plate to the novices' table. They are, after all, children, and children love chocolate cake ... don't they? And I can have the Khunying's cake anytime ... this succulent recipe that brings in a million baht a year.

In my room, I notice, suddenly, that the clock by my bed is upside down. That explains the confusion over time. It *was* the wee hours before dawn when I woke from that peculiar dream, and that is why I seemed to have overslept.

I sit in the mother-of-pearl chair, trying to analyze the dream. Though its basic meaning is pretty clear — my life has become a sacred place. Those who interfered with it in the past no longer belong. They can be sent away. The visit to Africa/Egypt has all sorts of mystical connotations, from the "darkest" Africa of my childhood adventure novels to the Egyptian symbology of death and resurrection. A rug is a relationship ... one that has proved, it seems, too expensive to be worth continuing. The ancient temple dug up stone by stone and moved to the new setting ... that must be the ancient wisdom that has now been transplanted into the landscape of my new consciousness. And the kids, expelled from this new paradise ... that too is obvious, indeed so fraught with symbolic logic as to seem to have been cooked up by a novelist. Well, look who's talking.

Using images from the unconscious mind to teach my conscious mind important lessons — is this what my attempts at the sleeping meditation are beginning to achieve? If so, it is surely about time. The human psyche so frequently walls off parts of itself from other parts. Lines of communication are weak. I'm very encouraged. I seem to have blown open a channel and forced the people inside me to talk to each other.

I've blown open another kind of channel as well, this morning; something has disagreed with me, and an upset stomach keeps me from attending morning chapel. Indeed, the Seer tells me I'd better not go to meditation class at all this morning; I wouldn't want to have a little accident while off in an adjacent universe.

The Seer insists that I take plenty of medicine and sends word to the Guru that his recalcitrant new monk won't show up this morning. I do hope that the Guru won't be annoyed. There is, you see, a subtle tension between the two, although I have not yet learned enough of the temple's politics to get all the nuances.

Now, all day long, people inquire about my upset stomach, even people I have never seen. Later I am told that the Guru has announced my diarrhea to the entire throng of meditation students. Imagine that happening at my old English boarding school! I would be the butt of jokes for weeks. But here, there is the greatest concern.

One monk after another comes to my room to show sympathy. One particular monk shows up at my door with a herbal remedy in his hand. This monk is very youthful, pale, always staring off into the distance, and he tells me that he knows things about me that others do not know.

"For instance," he tells me, "I know that you can see into the heart of the Guru, and that you have sensed a certain darkness there ... I know because I have seen it myself ... but we won't speak of it, because it's enough that we both know it is true."

It is a strange thing for one man to say to another as he presents him with herbal remedies for diarrhea, but this monk is unusual. Thais do not like to say things directly; they speak in understatement and misdirection, out of the desire to protect others from losing face, out of a fear of losing face themselves; this monk says things straight out, insightful things that perhaps one would rather not speak about.

He sees things. I tell him I have a friend who sees things — I'm talking about Sharon, on her mountaintop in Georgia, and the spirit Tomm who seems to speak through her. "Yes," he says, "I understand that completely. And you are like that, too."

I don't want to say that I'm very doubtful that I have any such abilities, so I simply smile. I will call this monk the Psychic. He is a new monk, but appears very otherworldly, as though he spends large chunks of his existence exploring other dimensions. He tells me that he has a genuine relic of the Lord Buddha in his room, and invites me to go and see it one day, when I'm feeling better.

I'm deeply moved at the gentility and compassion everyone shows towards me. There is also a certain chivalry that is rarely evident in the world outside, a certain profound respect for personhood; this is a community that lives by the principle of compassion.

During the lunch break, my parents show up; my dad will return to San Francisco tomorrow. My mother has brought the housekeeper from home, and insists that she clean my bathroom; she's worried because she doesn't think I'll succeed in doing it myself. A professional is needed. But there are problems, as a woman may not touch certain objects used by monks — "intimate" objects such as towels. At first, my mother tries to put away the towels herself, but our family chauffeur, who once served time in a monastery himself as a novice, tells her that the monkly towels are out of bounds.

In the afternoon, I rush back to meditation class to discover the walking meditation in full swing. Unable to find an unobtrusive spot to walk back and forth, I am compelled to traverse the very platform where the Guru himself is sitting, lost in some transcendental state upon his sermonizing chair. It is very strange. As I walk slowly back and forth, I close my eyes, trying to measure out the steps by feel alone ... wondering if this is how the blind walk ...

trying to feel the space by some means of extrasensory perception.

But it is hard to concentrate. I imagine that Big Brother, in the form of the Guru, is peering down at me from his High Chair. And of course, behind him, there is also the towering golden Buddha of the beatific, enigmatic and utterly tranquil smile. And I admit that it is a little scary, and I can't find that tranquil spot within myself at all. I imagine the Guru's baleful stare and I squeeze my eyes tight shut and hope for the buzzer to go off soon ... the buzzer which, like an oven timer, tells me that it will soon be time to come out of my meditative state.

Of course, the Guru probably isn't even staring, balefully or otherwise. But I feel it nonetheless, like an overactive superego.

Later on there is the sitting meditation, too — thirty minutes of it — but someone it doesn't feel quite as long as before. I must be getting used to it after all. My body is still not entirely attuned to it all, but there has clearly been improvement.

And still later, I get myself into a deep conversation with my fellow sufferer, the Skeptic. It turns out that he has major issues with what the Guru has been saying which go to the most basic concepts in Buddhism — the true nature of reincarnation, for instance. I myself do not wish to argue the niceties of philosophy. I don't want to know how many angels can dance on the head of a pin. I only want to know that they do in fact dance. That, I suppose, is the major difference between us.

The time comes for the evening meditation and now I find myself standing in the outer vihara under the stars — what passes for the stars in Bangkok — and all of sudden comes a light sprinkle, which, as I begin the walking meditation, turns into a storm. Thunder and lightning and a raging wind, yet somehow I don't find myself running into the cloister to seek shelter. I keep my eyes closed, I keep walking. This time, Big Brother is not watching. *Bud-dho, Bud-dho,* I repeat in my mind, the mantra for stilling the inner storm. It doesn't work. I walk. Rain flecks my face. It is beautiful; the air is pungent with the smell of crushed jasmine. I taste it on my lips. The wind whips against my robes. I feel all these things and revel in them, yet I am also very far away.

It is not the word *Bud-dho, buddho* that keeps ringing in my ears. Instead I hear a voice that whispers again and again a phrase from T.S. Eliot's *Four Quartets :* "the still point of the turning world." It is this motif that helps me to locate my inner center, and not some Pali mantra. Over and over these words sound in my inner ear, the "t"-sounds of *still* and *point* and *turning* punctuating the mantra much like drops of rain.

Can a poem by a Bostonian-turned-Englishman really substitute for the ineffable name of the Enlightened One as a formula for inner peace? I do not know, but I am already aware from my study of the Guru's teaching that words are in themselves nothing more than the empty air. It is not the words that precipitate the states of inner mindfulness. The Guru has said that even simple words like "in, out" or counting from one to five would work, if only the mind is ready for them to work. But for my over-educated cranium the Buddha comes to me in the voice of T.S. Eliot, and then, later, in words from the King James Bible — for the voice that whispers the words of Eliot seems to me to be none other than the "still, small voice" alluded to in the Old Testament. Is it hubris to believe that such mighty powers might be speaking directly to oneself? I do not know. Buddhism does not, in the end, believe that such mighty forces are real; like the corporeal world itself, they too are parts of a great dream, though perhaps from a higher plane of dreaming than our concrete cosmos.

I feel myself detaching from my body. I feel myself at the eye of the tempest. The world rages; I am calm. I know that I have been searching for this stillness for a long time. But the stillness has stolen up to me, has ambushed me; I am so surprised to be holding the grail in my hands, even for a fleeting moment, that before I am aware of it, I have already let go.

When I was a child, I was in love with the wind. I felt that the wind spoke to me. I had a very strange adventure with the wind once; I wrote a poem about the wind when I was eleven, which poem ended up, by a strange string of coincidences, being published in the Bangkok *Post*. Even more oddly, the American actress Shirley MacLaine was passing through

Bangkok at that moment, and for some reason the poem seemed to make an impression on her, although she did not apparently know it was by some child. Perhaps the very awkwardness of its expression made it look as though it were the inadequately translated work of some ancient sage. Or perhaps, with the instinct so many artists seem to possess, she saw past the silly words straight into the soul of an alienated, anguished child.

Be that as it may, years later the poem about the wind appeared as the epigraph to Ms. MacLaine's autobiography, *Don't Fall off the Mountain,* and my childish words about the wind have sold more copies than all my "real" books put together.

Mistaken for an ancient sage at 11, here I am now, perhaps trying to pass myself off as a sage after a few days of monkhood! There are ironies here to be sure. I once told this story to a reporter for a well-known psychic magazine in the States, and she said, "Well, since that Shirley MacLaine book can fairly be said to have kicked off the New Age, that makes you the godfather of the entire New Age, doesn't it?" Scary.

But seriously now, there are things all children know, things they forget when they pass through the flames of adolescence and enter the grownup world, where imagination must sit in the back of the bus, where the touchable is confused with the real. These things we knew as children can be rediscovered as adults, but often only at the end of arduous voyages or after much pain.

The wind that whispered to me in my childhood and gave birth to a rather dreadful poem has spoken to me again, and this time I recognize it as a friend, and am almost ready to call it by name.

When I return to the vihara for the sitting meditation, the wind is still carrying on outside. I decide to continue my communion with nature. Resolutely, I pick up one of the little plastic chairs I have been using to meditate in, and place it by the window. A gorgeous window, paneled wood, black and gold lacquerwork, covered with images of gods and demons; it is ajar, and I push it wider, thinking, here, in the safety of the vihara yet exposed to the roar of the wind, I will once more hear the voice of God.

But wind does not help me at all. It howls, it batters my face. I am hopelessly distracted.

Profound inner experiences, it seems, can neither be manufactured nor preordained. I don't think I'll sit to meditate in a howling wind again … after all, didn't Buddha himself say no to self-mortification and return to the Middle Way in order to achieve enlightenment?

*Day Six*

# Buddhist-Style Politics

We proceed from an arcane discussion of *Vipassana,* the art of meditating on the nature of reality, to political chaos. It is almost the last day of the crash course in meditation, and, having emerged from a forty-minute session of contemplating the universe, we students now turn to contemplating each other.

The Guru announces, on our emerging from the inner world, that the meditation class is going to have a big "event" on the last day — with the awarding of certificates and other fanfare — and that it is necessary to elect a committee to run the event. What's more, the committee in charge of the event will also be a subcommittee of the entire association of ex-meditation students of this course, a group comprising several thousand people, and will meet from time to time during the year to organize events and follow up everyone's progress towards enlightenment.

You must imagine my bewilderment at this announcement. For almost a week now, I have spent about six hours a day in the company of some three hundred meditators. But I have barely exchanged a word with any of them. As a monk, as one of only two monks registered for this course, I have not socialized with the meditation students; I have tended to go straight from the vihara to my kuti each afternoon, to spend even more hours in contemplation. Nor have the meditators really communicated with me; since I am a monk, my exchanges with them have consisted of little more than politely acknowledging their obeisance as they pass me on bended knee, on their way to their individual meditation cushions, scattered around the vihara.

The Guru answers my unspoken question as he addresses the throng from his preaching chair.

"Most of you don't know each other, barely talk to each other, and never met before signing up for this course," he tells us. "But, you see, there is a directory of all the meditation students available." This mimeographed book is now being handed out to all the participants; it is a twenty-page document, with names, addresses, and serial numbers for each of us, beginning with the two monks — I for instance am student number two.

The entire list is read aloud, and names are quickly put to faces. But it's pretty much a whirlwind election campaign; each one of us gets about five seconds of perfunctory appraisal from the others.

"What I want all of you to do," says the Guru, "after the lunch break, is to look through this directory and study the names. There will be a nominating period where any of you will be able to name whoever you want to the committee, and your votes will be approved by a show of hands. Then, the committee will go off and elect a chairman, vice-chairman, treasurer and so on, who will then draw up the order of the day for tomorrow's festivities. Last year's committee will be on hand to assist this year's. So — best of luck, and may many blessings descend upon this year's administrative committee."

A little voice pipes up from somewhere in the crowd. "But, honored teacher ... how will we know whom to nominate? We don't know anything about anyone's qualifications."

"Oh, don't worry about it," the Guru responds. "It will all work out. Now, off with you all to lunch."

As I slip out of the vihara, a young lady shyly asks me, her nose still buried in the mimeographed directory, whether I am S.P. Somtow, the writer. I have of course been trying to remain anonymous here, but, as a monk, I cannot lie, so I am forced to plead guilty. She giggles slightly, then disappears into the shadows. It is the first time since my entering this cloistered world that anyone has mentioned my career beyond the walls.

I see now that people are in fact worming their way through the directory, gazing at names and numbers.

The Guru himself does not have lunch. He remains on this throne, in the vihara, taking questions from those who remain behind; outside, in the canvas monks' pavilion that has been set up to shield us from the blazing sun, I am told by one of the monks from the Guru's *kuti* that he never eats lunch. "He is so holy," he tells me, "that he is able to eat only one meal a day."

On the other hand, the Guru is hardly skinny, so I imagine that he must be getting all his food groups each morning.

Thailand is famous for bewildering elections, and the one that follows the lunch break is a splendid example. There is no one in charge per se, but somehow it manages to muddle through. "All right," the Guru announces. "Before you start meditating again, let's start the nominations process. For the next fifteen minutes, let anyone who wishes to nominate someone raise his hand and announce their candidate's serial number, and we will have a show of hands to see whether the rest of you consent to the nomination."

There are no Robert's Rules of Order, no standardized parliamentary procedures, and nobody really knows anybody else. But, after a few awkward moments, some scattered hands go up.

Number 212. Will Number 212 please make himself known? Do we all approve? About a hundred signal their assent.

And so it goes on. People are nominated — everyone gets chosen. Nobody loses face. How they know who to nominate eludes me. And yet everyone's polite, there's no pushing and shoving, and by the end of the process everyone's clearly having a good time.

To my astonishment, the young lady who earlier has asked me whether I am indeed *the* S.P. Somtow now raises her hand and nominates "Number Two", and — unanimously, it appears — I am elected to this ad hoc committee. Next, someone nominates Number One, who as it happens is my friend the Intellectual Monk — and he too becomes a member of this administrative body.

And I still have no clue what it is we're supposed to be administrating.

All this takes perhaps twenty minutes. The Guru calls down the blessing of karma and divinities on the committee's deliberations to come; then he announces that all the students will meditate for forty-five minutes — all except for the committee, who will now adjourn for forty-five minutes to make all the preparations for tomorrow's graduation ceremony.

I have been dreading the forty-five minutes all day, and it is with some relief that I hitch up my robes and go to the committee meeting, which is in fact occupied with another election.

The head of last year's committee gives a speech. "Here's the deal," he tells us. "You need a president, a vice-president or two, a treasurer, assistant treasurer, secretary, head of publicity, and various other positions. Once that's done, you present the list to the Guru, and he signs off on it, and the list is beautifully printed up as part of the credits for the memory-book of this meditation session. You'll need to confer about photographers, collecting donations, and other details. The nuns will handle the catering."

I'm still suffering from the delusion that this committee is actually supposed to work in a businesslike fashion to run this event. So I ask why we don't streamline the whole process, put one or two people in charge instead of this enormous board, and do the whole thing like a proper corporation.

But our advisor pooh-poohs this overly western line of reasoning. "That's impossible," he says. "For one thing, the Guru will not sign off on the list of board members unless every single position has a name attached to it, because it won't match the list of previous years. Secondly, you guys don't actually have to do anything per se; we, who handled the event last year and the year before, will actually do all the work."

The committee therefore proceeds to assign itself exalted positions — there are no privates in this army, everyone's a general. The upshot of it is that I am voted Vice President for Foreign Affairs — and given wide-ranging authority to deal with any situation that may arise should tomorrow's big event encounter any international diplomatic crises. I accept the position with respect and humility, as it is offered to me in all seriousness.

Suddenly, I realize that this whole thing isn't about putting on tomorrow's show at all. It is rather, in fact, a clever ploy for this motley group of students, who have already spent almost a week in the same vihara, each one isolated in his little meditative bubble, to begin interacting on a social level, to begin a process of networking that will continue after the meditation course is over.

For we end the session with this warm fuzzy camaraderie that wasn't there before. Even those who voted for me by acclamation, who have never spoken to me, now have a connection to me, and I to them.

As we troop back into the vihara, the insight hits me. I've been thinking all this time that we have been running around in circles and achieving very little. But I was wrong. This is no longer a ragtag assemblage of individuals; we have bonded, we're a sort of team.

The whole point of the exercise has been the process, not the foreordained result. The journey's destination is the journey itself.

Once more, I have witnessed Buddhism at work, ever elusive, ever subtle, ever compassionate. Tomorrow will be the acid test — will this strange committee actually get anything done? I can't wait to find out.

*Day Seven*

# Plagued by Doubts

Day Seven begins with gravest doubts. Partly it's because yesterday's late night lecture seemed to both of us new monks to be superstitious and bizarre; partly, I think, because of aches and pains — my arthritis really getting to me, for instance. I am certainly feeling the discomfiture of the flesh, which is a lesson being drummed into me daily. My feet are burning; my stomach is churning.

I know that I dreamed vividly last night, yet have no recollection now, just flashes of color. I wake up and — oddly enough — experience little difficulty with the robes, for once; I am on a sort of autopilot. This is worrying. Monks shouldn't be on autopilot. They should absorb every experience as though it were unique. Which in point of fact, it is.

This should be a glorious day — I am graduating from the weeklong meditation course with a fine certificate and, besides, I have now been elected Vice-President of this magnificent committee that will oversee the coming festivities. But my friend, the Intellectual, has been regaling me with his doubts; and I must admit that doubt torments me, too.

The Guru, you see, was telling the faithful supplicants that there are certain loopholes in the Five Precepts which all Buddhists are asked to observe. (Contravening these precepts is not sin in the Judaeo-Christian sense, but it may lead, perhaps, to a negative progression in one's karmic journey.) "Let's suppose," the Guru has been telling us, "that you are sitting in a room, and the mosquitoes are starting to become a nuisance. You desperately want to slap a few, and eventually you open fire with the old aerosol, leaving a dozen dead souls on the floor. And so you've destroyed a dozen lives just because of your momentary annoyance. But what if you didn't *intend* to kill them — what if you offer them a way out? Let's say you leave a window ajar, and instead of letting fly with the airborne poison, you just spray a bit here, a bit there, like a delicate sort of farting? You will have annoyed the mosquitoes, and most will choose to depart through the window ... and those who do in fact end up whizzing, open-winged, into the embrace of the fumes, well then it's their own karma, not yours, since you did not spray to kill, but simply to ... influence their choices a little."

At lunch the other day, I have been saying, "Yeah, that may be a loophole, but some of those insects are just as dead as in the other scenario. And no matter what you *say* you intend, you're still trying to get rid of them and you still have a bit of the executioner's motives clinging to your mind."

A monk I have not yet met, tall and pale, somewhat older than the new monks, says, "There are really three different levels of moral law. The first is the law as laid down by humans, the most imperfect. The second is the law embodied in the precepts or *silas*, such as that we must refrain from taking life ... but what you say brings us to a third level of moral law: the law of *dhamma*, which allows even less wiggle room than the others...."

The previous night, the Guru has repeated the maxim about the mosquitoes to the throng. It's obviously a very meaningful thing to him. But it has given me a sleepless night.

What torments me most? I suppose it's the Guru's assertion that there are lawyerly loopholes in the dharma. That there is the possibility that one could spray a little bit of insect repellent without *intending* to kill any mosquitoes, and that by judiciously willing them to fly out of the window, one is not really breaking the first precept of Buddhism — to refrain from taking life.

Are we splitting hairs here, or discussing ultimate truth?

It seems, perhaps, to be a little melodramatic, but I have this flashing image of the infamous Wahnsee Conference — the big meeting over sixty years ago in which, with chilling banality, the bigwigs of the Nazi party discussed the mechanics of the Final Solution. I mean, to a good Buddhist, every soul is equally valuable, whether a mosquito or a human; every soul is a fellow-traveler on the same journey. And so, I have this horrible vision of mosquitoes huddling in mosquito ghettoes, overhearing us "enlightened" human beings as we decide that if they just happen to stumble into poison gas that we've cunningly deployed, we're blameless of their deaths.

Mosquitoes have stung me, but they have never given me nightmares before. I realize now that this has something to with the vivid dreams that I dare not bring back to memory.

And yet, walking out of the monastery with my begging bowl, I am astonished to find the bowl miraculously filled within about two minutes by a small group of faithful people, and I walk back, laden with offerings, realizing that these people's simple faith in the karmic power of their gift to me has probably made them feel blessed and hopeful. What, then, is more important — the elaborate structure of levels of reality and truth, with their myriad Pali names — or this simple belief that goodness will return goodness?

Lunch is chaotic, with a lot of relatives showing up, and delicious honey roasted pork (I'm not allowed to say it's delicious, of course, at the time, but now I can) and then the evening is again one of those delightfully Thai occasions, the presenting of the meditation diplomas; the Guru on his high chair, much crawling about and respectful folding of palms. Much taking of photographs, too, and everyone beaming; the whole vihara seems to float on a cumulus of joy.

Finally, the Guru commands the monks to go outside and meditate, but they're actually all chatting and drinking chrysanthemum tea when I emerge. Chattering away mostly in a Southern dialect which sounds as melodious to me as would the genteel drawl of a Georgia gentlewoman. There are more photos to be taken, anecdotes and addresses to be exchanged ... and then — the horror! — a few more people among the devotees have figured out that the mysterious monk in the background who hardly dares show his face is in reality the writer S.P. Somtow. Finally, the outside world has begun to impinge. And it's today, as it were the very midpoint in this very brief journey, that I begin to have thoughts of returning to the world beyond.

There really *is* a world beyond. And I am beginning to hear its call. To hear, but not to heed; I know, I sense, that the second week will be the time of real confrontations with the darkness and the demons of selfhood. The first week has been all pep rallies and light, really; tomorrow the three hundred meditators will have gone home, and there will just be us, the New Monks, and the temple, and the odyssey that does not even take a break to sleep, for our newly lucid dreams carry us onward to ever more remote stations in the journey.

The ad hoc committee has done a miraculous job. A slight problem arises when my co-sufferer and I want to donate 500 baht (about $15) to the meditation course's slush fund.  Of course, as monks, we possess no money, cannot even, in fact, touch money.  We decide to ask the treasurer to put money in on our behalf, and to collect it from us the day after we return to our lay existences.

Despite the Intellectual's doubts — and they are clearly very legitimate — it is clear that the course has had its benefits.  I see everything much more clearly, and my ability to visualize during meditation has become stronger.  But right now, I don't want to meditate again for a long time.  Well, at least, not until tomorrow.

That evening, I am summoned by the Guru to sit in meditation once more, but I am so exhausted from an entire week of concentrated meditation that I can barely respond.  No, no, no more meditation!  I think to myself ... yet how can I avoid the Guru's summons?

It seems to me, however, that I am saved by a stroke of karma from another evening of self-mortification.

You see, I have taken the opportunity to wash both of my robes, and since there is no such thing here as a dryer, they are still wet, hanging up to dry.

I tell the Little Novice who has come to fetch me the reason I can't leave my room — and he says to me, "Funny!   The other New Monk had the same excuse."

Is it serendipity or cosmic planning?

*Day Eight*
# Killing the Sacred Cows

A curiously vivid dream at dawn after the reclining meditation; this time it is very unclear. We are ancient Romans and there is a civil war going on. I lead a small group of people to investigate the enemy, who appears to be led by a certain Minos. At one point, we are riding a train, and I know that the enemy has no train. "What color are Minos's bulls?" I ask aloud. It might be better to sacrifice some cattle rather than have the battle. I find four bulls, one black, one brown, two ... can't remember. Our small unit drives the bulls into the hills beside the castle of the enemy; then we conceal ourselves, but discuss the matter loudly enough for a spy to hear. Then, arrows begin to rain down from the sky. Each pierces a cow or bull; they die quietly, quickly, without fuss, sort of melting away; each one is completely weightless, a phantom. Dozens of them are being pierced and falling dead and vanishing. Then, I escape down to the river. Again, there's a mode of transportation that the enemy doesn't have; a car, I think, perhaps a Jaguar ... and I drive away as I wake up.

What was all that about? It's time to kill the sacred cows, perhaps? In other words, only by removing one's most cherished beliefs can one actually "escape" the civil war? Clearly the civil war represents some kind of inner conflict, and some of the imagery seems borrowed from my own science fiction books.

I am entirely alone this morning in my begging; perhaps it's because I left early. I don't see any well-wishers about at all, but as I walk into the marketplace, miraculously, the bowl becomes rapidly very full. The *khai tun* that only yesterday I have gazed upon longingly in someone else's tray of offerings, by a stroke of karma, now appears in my own alms-bowl. Is this an answer to an unspoken prayer, or is it a coincidence? I remember that Sharon Webb, the psychic, once told me that there are no coincidences in the worlds. That we make our own reality. Now, that is also exactly what Buddha said — that heaven and hell can be states within our own consciousness. When asked whether such states exist objectively, he avoided answering directly; but then, in the Buddhist view of the universe, there is no objective reality at all. Existence itself is an illusion made concrete by our clinging to it, by our desire for it.

Worried, perhaps, that I'll starve to death with the unfamiliar food, famous philanthropist and opera producer Dr. Suprija shows up in the morning to present me with a huge roast beef, garlic bread, and other marvels of European cooking from the kitchen of his wife, one of Thailand's most famous gourmands. He also presents me with crepes and Haagen-Dazs ice cream. Then, my uncle and aunt show up with a huge steak ... having the same idea that I'm going to die without familiar foods. What an abundance of largesse!

Alas, there is no one with whom to share this. All the other monks in the kuti have gone elsewhere for lunch. I sit in the Seer's dining room in solitary monkly splendor. I cannot invite the laywomen who so lovingly set out the food to join me at my table; I cannot even engage them in chit-chat; I must carefully, thoughtfully, chew this exquisite repast while meditating constantly on the fact that life is illusion, that the flavors and textures of this fine exemplar of *haute cuisine* are but distractions from the journey toward enlightenment.

How many of the 227 precepts discuss eating? One must not take large mouthfuls, must not eat noisily or with gusto, must not ... if this sounds like a excerpt from Miss Manners's etiquette book, well, there is an element of that. To be a monk is to be endlessly self-effacing, endlessly polite. Even the rules on chewing are part of the discipline.

I worry that all this fine cuisine will go to waste, but I am assured that the food could in fact be re-offered a day later without breaking the spirit of the monastic vows. And so, making sure that the ice cream is saved for the Littlest Novice, I leave the lonely luncheon and return to my chamber to meditate.

In the afternoon, I go for my first extended visit outside the walls of the monastery, to visit an aged aunt who is unable to travel.

It is my first sally into the outside world, except for the visits to the market across the street with my begging bowl.  I put on my robe (completely covering both shoulders as is customary for leaving the temple) and set forth in my mother's chauffeur-driven Mercedes, which has arrived to bring me to my aunt's house.

It is a curiously moving afternoon. My relatives are there in force, but view me differently.  I feel a little bit like Tom Sawyer spying on his own funeral; the person I thought I was is dead, is spoken of in the third person; I am a kind of ghost.  In my high seat, I seem to float above them as they gingerly bring me a glass of ice water on bended knee.  We talk of ordinary things: of people's health, of whether there will be floods.  Yet there is a strange ritualistic quality to our conversations, as though we are rehearsing a drama that has played out a million times since the beginning of history.  It is not exactly an unreality — more a heightened reality, in which every little thing seems to have added meaning.

As I leave, however, I realize I have not yet learned the proper ritual formula for blessing the people I visit. I am worried. I do not want my aunt to be disappointed. But she says she is not.

"It is a blessing," she tells me, "to see my nephew in the yellow robe before I die."

Later, the Jao Khun looks at my horoscope, and determines that I shall leave the monastery on the Tuesday 21$^{st}$ — the exact 15$^{th}$ day after I entered. There will be a feast, he suggests, and my family could offer food to the entire monastery in celebration.

He then tells me that my assignment for the week will be to compose a sermon — in English, he agrees, much to my relief — and deliver it to an audience of relatives and interested parties within the next 5-6 days. The text of the sermon will be printed out and made into a Thai and English booklet, to be kept around as a handout. Pretty frightening, eh! In my many years as a churchgoing member of the C. of E., I never had to do anything like that!

I have a project now, it seems. I realize that the Seer has done this, not because the sermon I preach will be some masterful interpretation of Buddhist philosophy, but to help me to focus in the coming week. After all, what will people really learn about the ultimate truth from someone who has only been a monk for eight days? But preparing the sermon will purify my mind.

Now comes the time for the evening chanting, and today for the first time the Guru, freed from the onus of the weeklong meditation course, decides to lead the prayers personally. He chants very beautifully (and very slowly) thus inflaming my joints to a horrifying degree. Then, at the end, he delivers an absolutely fascinating speech in which he analyses King Rama IV's skill in creating chants in the Pali language. The speech is so interesting that I'm in severe conflict with the pain of maintaining the phabphieb position considered so becoming in a monk. By the end of the speech, I have developed huge bruises on my knees. Life, of course, is suffering; such is only a matter of degree.

Evening meditation is in the *kuti* of the abbot. The pain is unbelievable as there are no chairs, and I fail to achieve the kind of wondrous *piti* that characterized my sessions in the vihara itself. I try to say over and over in my mind, "There is no pain, there is no pain."

And so — this being something in the nature of a confessional — I admit that I am as far from a state of samadhi as one can imagine. I am distracted. My mind floats. And then — I cheat. I peek. In the tiny outer room of the abbot's *kuti*, surrounded by gorgeous hand-painted murals of the Chinese Romance of the Three Kingdoms, a dozen monks are sitting in absolute stillness. I can feel their collective breath, I can sense their inner quietude, and I feel like an intruder. What am I doing here? I am a shadow hiding in their shadow, and they themselves are distant shadows cast by a two-thousand-year-old Indian prince who demanded an answer to the problem of suffering.

At the end of the hour, my leg has gone to sleep, and when the meditation is over I can't quite get up. I have to be helped up by several of my fellow New Monks. It is a little embarrassing, but everyone is very helpful.

Well, I know that the purpose of all this is *not* self-torture. I will attempt some other way to deal with the problem tomorrow night. Perhaps a rearrangement of the floor cushions.

*Day Nine*

# The Psychic

Day Nine begins with the usual *pintapada*; I leave a little later than usual because I have been told that it's inadvisable to leave before the dawn is actually pink. Yesterday, when I left really early and my bowl was crammed with good things by well-wishers, was apparently a bending of the rules, though in my ignorance I had not realized that. One should not leave the *kuti* until it is actually dawn, for the stricture against eating solid food lasts from the moment the sun is high in the sky all the way until the first rays of the sun arise in the east.

It has been raining; the feel of the wet streets on my feet, slippery and oily ... there is a certain harshness until one remembers how much the earliest monks must have suffered, walking down unpaved pathways along stony ground, through mud and slush; what I endure is nothing.

After morning chapel, the young monk known as the Psychic comes to my *kuti*. He speaks of mental powers developed through meditation. He is a young man, who has dedicated three months of his life to the monkhood because of his father, who is about to have a heart valve operation. "You must come to my *kuti*," he tells me. "I've got all sorts of interesting relics. I have an actual relic of the Lord Buddha himself … in a little vial … you can touch it, feel its power."

Also, he tells me, "I was unemployed, struggling, for two years … and now I'm at peace." He tells me that he can see into my soul, and he sees that, like him, I have the ability to read the abbot's heart; "but," he says to me, "we shan't speak of it." He says, "I only say this to you because I can already tell that you already know it." It's a rather roundabout way of discussing things, but I think we both end up knowing what the other is trying to say.

He tells me that he has studied reflexology and used to give sessions for 250 baht. His ambition is to go to India and to visit all the sites where the Buddha lived and taught.

Lunch is that wonderful roast beef that was brought over by the owner of Bangkok's famous The Cup restaurant.

This afternoon, I am supposed to spend some time at the Buddhist school, learning a few things.

We will see what will happen. Well ... I have to say that the learning method is what might be called very primitive, by Western standards; there is a textbook on the life of the Buddha, and students take turns reading from it, and the Jao Khun who teaches then expounds on the book's meaning. There is little opportunity for discussion. And yet it is moving to see the people in the classroom, who range in age from 13 to 49, all studiously following text and listening raptly to the venerable teacher.

Then, Nop Sotthibandu, a famous Thai composer, drops in. Nop is a pupil of the famed guru Sai Baba, and a disciple of Krishna. We have a fascinating discussion about Buddhism and its relationship with Krishna consciousness; perhaps, I think, it is a more fruitful discussion than the one that is presently going on in the classroom. The oddest part of it is this: in the classroom, we have been reading about Buddha's disciple Ananda's questions to the Lord Buddha as he was about to enter Nirvana; during the middle of the talk with Ajarn Nop, he starts to tell me the next piece of Ananda's conversation with Buddha ... even though he had no idea that was what was being discussed! It was as if I was miraculously continuing the lesson even after it ended!

It is perfectly clear to me that the classroom, the *kuti*, all the external appurtenances of this monastery are a kind of psychological crutch. Reality itself is a crutch, of course; that is the essence of Buddhism. The true journey is taking place inside the mind. If a lesson is not completed in the words of one teacher, it continues out of the mouth of another. Identities, locations, times are all melding into one another, into a single internal landscape.

I am slowly beginning to learn that the world within these walls is not bounded by the laws of physics. Well, not entirely, at any rate.

The outer world intrudes once more as I attempt to print something out on this computer, involving bringing over equipment from the house, discovering that the *kuti* has incompatible plugs, and other technological problems.

After an hour or two of frustration, I realize that I *could* just let go. I am, after all, a monk right now. I don't have any urgency. The cosmic journey lasts many lifetimes.

After chapel, the tall monk has many questions and also a book to give me. He is a fascinating person, quite a character; he's written a few books full of pithy sayings and short reflective pieces about Buddhism.

Evening meditation lasts 30 minutes. Only getting brief flashes of *piti*; once again, it's the arthritis. The abbot's *kuti* has no accessible chairs, so I really am forced to attempt "the position."

The second night in a row, I have trouble sleeping. In the morning, there comes a possible answer: I have set the day of my departure incorrectly, and thus disturbed the underlying forces of my karma.

I will not be allowed to leave until astrology dredges up a more auspicious date.

*Day Ten*

# The Hound of Heaven

In the morning comes an urgent call from my mother. Would it be possible for me to leave the monastery on Wednesday instead of Tuesday?

She has been told by a Chinese nun, via my sister, that Tuesday would be inappropriate because of bad astrological portents, and that it is also against Chinese custom to do such a thing on Tuesday.

This Chinese nun lives in a sampan. Well, sort of. Her dwelling is made of concrete and would sink like — well, like concrete — were it ever to put to sea. Her dwelling is some kind of symbol. We are on a perpetual voyage. I call her the Prophesying Nun and later I will tell you about how she believes one's karma should be tagged, color-coded … but that is for a later chapter.

Thailand is full of miraculous nuns, including a famous floating one, but this is one who lives in a boat that does *not* float.

I can see many fine metaphors in this boat. It is permanently anchored to the earth. It is unsinkable, because it has already sunk. It represents illusion.

The nun's "consultations" — which I once took on my sister's insistence — consist of making one take a nap within a cabin of the boat. "Do you *dare* to go to sleep there?" she will ask. As though a profound vision, life-changing and epiphanic, was bound to come. I experienced no such thing: could not even get to sleep, the floor was so hard. Personally, I think she's probably a charlatan, but one must be polite to Prophesying Nuns, just in case.

I feel that I should satisfy everyone's astrological concerns, and as a monk, I cannot really refuse a reasonable request. So I agree. Therefore, this diary may be a little longer than originally planned!

The thoughtful young psychic monk has returned. I am sitting in my room, composing this journal. He's considerate, doesn't want to intrude, but I also see a burning desire to communicate; he seems to see a kindred soul. He really wants to tell me something, but I put him off, feeling rather guilty about it, since I should not really be thinking about myself.

Afternoon: I go to visit the sick and attempt to practice *ubhekha*.

My aunt is very ill.  My mother picks me up and we go to the hospital, where she perhaps is dying.

This is how it goes down.  My aunt is lying in a hospital bed.  It is a luxurious room — they are well off — it is well lit, with nice drapes, and the life is draining away from her; she can no longer speak. Not that she ever spoke much.  Or rather, she did speak, in rapid outbursts, like a speeded-up cartoon character.   Very few people could actually understand anything she said, but actually it wasn't hard; you simply had to retain each utterance and then stretch it out, as with an old reel to reel tape deck, play it back at 3 3/4 ips instead of 7 1/2, and then she sounded normal.

My aunt had Down's syndrome, you see. Raised with all sorts of caretakers and maids, she had in a sense a charmed life.  And while my family lives in a self-sustaining soap opera of Machiavellian intrigue, she alone was beyond all of it.  That is why I always loved her so much.

She lies there, quite helpless now, the luxury meaningless.  Her eyes are closed but now and then her lips make snapping noises.

They leave me along with her in the room.  As a monk, I cannot even lay hands on her; touching a woman would violate the 227 precepts.  What I feel is a vast helplessness. I am here to give comfort, perhaps, but I can't.

It is a terrible moment, and yet in a strange way uplifting.

Evening chapel....

The Psychic has a secret admirer, one of the temple dogs. This particular dog doesn't miss an opportunity to climb onto the monk's robes and start thrusting passionately. He is fixated on this one monk — there must be some personal odor or something that drives the dog wild with passion. We keep wondering why this dog is so in love. After evening chapel, the dog is waiting patiently by the gate, and when the object of his passion emerges from chapel, he trots after him, dare I say it, doggedly. The Psychic finds this dog amusing, but I think he's also beginning to find his attentions a little tiresome. Not to mention peculiar. However, as monks, we spread our compassion to all creatures who share our world. Even a lovesick, leprous dog.

Night falls: The Abbot, our Guru, has gone to Phuket, but we continue to meet for meditation practice in his *kuti*. It's a little less painful tonight. Perhaps it's just that the Guru isn't watching.

# Brahmavihara:
## The Noble States of Mind

Here's another "magic four" to go along with recollections, mindfulnesses, and noble truths. It seems that the number four is vital in Buddhism, as it is in alchemy (earth, air, water, fire) or ancient medicine (the four humors) or in music (the string quartet, some would say, is the ultimate expression of purity in classical music.)

Brahmavihara are four crucial concepts in Buddhism. Naturally, they have poetic names in Pali that defy exact translation. They are *metta, karuna, mudita,* and *upekkha.*

These four concepts, if one meditates upon them effectively enough, may, it is said, cause one to be reborn in one of the higher heavens, the heavens so high that the gods themselves can't reach them. When one looks at these four ideas, one realizes just how far apart the philosophical world of Buddhism is from the Judaeo-Christian one.

Christianity tells us that we must love one another. *Metta,* the first of the four concepts, is the closest to *agape* in the Christian sense, but it doesn't actually mean *love* at all. It's sometimes translated as loving-kindness or benevolence.

One of the most frequent of Buddhist rituals is *phae metta,* which means "spreading metta" — it is the act of projecting *metta* towards other creatures and the universe itself. When you see those monks sitting in lotus position doing nothing, that's often precisely what they are doing; adding, infinitesimally, to the universe's quotient of benevolence.

Crucially, the act of projecting loving-kindness into the cosmos also lowers the amount of negativity. So you may think that nothing is happening, but the monks would tell you otherwise.

*Karuna* is usually translated as *compassion.* According to the Pali scriptures, *metta* projects kindness onto others, while *karuna* seeks to take away others' suffering. In that sense its meaning is close to *compassion* which means the ability to *suffer* (passio) *with* (con-) another.

Then it starts to get complicated because *mudita* is the selfless joy that one feels at another's well-being.

Fair enough, but *upekkha* is usually translated as *equanimity* — the ability to be unaffected by loss and gain, resentment, happiness and grief and other emotions born out of our preoccupation with the illusion that is our world.

So while the Brahmavihara states of mind start with being acutely aware of others and feeling their pain, they end with detachment and letting go.

## Day Eleven
# Monk School

I spend the day composing my sermon. The Guru sends a message to us new monks, telling us to elect a chairman and organize a photo shoot, a sort of "Class of '01" group photo.

Lunch: the famous roast duck from the restaurant down the street is finally presented to the monks. The Seer says, "Everyone thinks we're always being presented with this succulent, famed duck because the restaurant is so close. So it hardly ever shows up here."

Jip Gee is the name of this establishment, and I never, in real life, get to visit it, simply because it's one of those places that, when they run out of duck, they just close; and they tend to run out by early afternoon, because they are so famous.

Today there are several supplicants who want an astrological reading. One of the monks whispered to me the other day, "How much does the Lord Seer charge for a reading?" He is reputed to be very rich because of his astrological brilliance. No one seems to remark that the Lord Seer shouldn't be taking money at all. Commerce and piety are mated for life.

Monk school: an unbelievably elaborate system is laid out of what to do and when and where to do it. Then, the Tall smiling monk tells us there's going to be a test on Monday. Since the test will be written, in Thai, I will probably find a way of sneaking away. After a lifetime of being the smartest kid in the class, it is astonishing, and humbling, to find myself, at this advanced age, the stupidest.

After school there is another wild election, democracy in action once more. Since I don't know the names of many of the monks, they decide to do it all by number, and there is a sort of secret ballot. This time I luck out — I don't get elected to any position whatsoever. Just as well!

Hardly anyone shows up for the evening chapel, but it seems that this is because the abbot has gone to Phuket. The Intellectual says to me, "When the cat's away, the mice will play." Since I haven't yet finished writing my sermon, I decide that I will forego the evening's meditation session. I mean, it's not doing me that much good these days, what with the pain. Now ... I am writing the last words of the sermon.

My mother calls to ask how to translate certain words. Even though the Seer has told me that it's fine to do the sermon in English, she thinks we should distribute a translation.

For the brilliant translator of *Jasmine Nights*, translating a Buddhist sermon ends up being quite problematic, because there's quite a bit of specialized vocabulary. Buddhism has its own terminology, like *mindfulness* and *detachment*, which don't have exact equivalents between Pali, Thai and English. So we struggle for a faithful translation.

*Day Twelve*

# Sacred Relics

The rhythm of the brooms across the stone courtyard steals over the music of the night. The cool monsoon rain has fallen all night long, and in the dawn the tiles glisten with residual moisture, gold, copper, vermilion. I don my robes for the morning almsgiving.

In the end, putting on the robes seems the most difficult thing in the universe. I have slowly begun to realize that there may well be no special trick to it … that those who are ahead of me in experience may well be having as much difficulty as I am, twisting the ends, twirling the join, flicking the arm-segment over the shoulder, poking, pulling, keeping the thing from falling off.

As I descend from the kuti the morning breeze, like a washcloth, swabs at my hands and face.

The stones of the street are sharp against my feet, and yet there are so many almsgivers in the marketplace that I can barely carry back their largesse. There is barely a hint of traffic. The marketplace, with its narrow walkways, its vendors setting up in the dawn, its baskets of virgin fruit, is like a whole world waiting to be born. In the chaos of my life's journey, I have stumbled upon an unexpected stillness.

A pile of chicken bones, heaped against the gutter, puts me in mind of my mortality.

My psychic friend has been speaking to me of his sacred relic ... an actual of the Lord Buddha himself ... though what kind of piece, I am uncertain. "I keep asking you if you want to come and see my relic of Lord Buddha," he says to me after morning chapel, "and you never come."

I must admit that I have been putting off this moment. Why? Because the idea of relics disturbs me. I think of the charlatan in the Canterbury Tales who, Chaucer tells us, passes off "pigges bones" as the relics of saints. I know that there are plenty such in the Buddhist community as well. The Psychic tells me that I'll never experience anything as miraculous as holding this relic in my hand. I am always dubious of such claims; I admit it to myself, but not to my friend. On the other hand, he *is* a psychic; he's told me so himself. He must realize I'm not entirely sure about it all.

The Psychic takes me to his chamber, which is in a different *kana* or section of the monastery. This *kana* consists of a row of rickety, stilted wooden houses in the traditional Thai style — quite different from the air-conditioned splendor in which I have been residing.

As we reach the veranda, I see clocks. Hundreds of clocks hang on the walls, not one of them telling the same time. There are chiming clocks, electric clocks, souvenir clocks. There are religious clocks, scenic clocks, miniature clocks, massive grandfather clocks. There are little cheap clocks that you get as free gifts from department stores, and expensive jeweled clocks.

He explains that the clocks all belong to his master, his Phra Khru, who has been collecting them for years. He shows me into his inner sanctum. It is a closet of a room, and the walls are completely covered with clocks, those most of them are no longer running, and again, here, not one tells the same time as another. A little bed leans against one wall. "That's not my bed," the Psychic says, "that's my Phra Khru's; I get a tatami on the floor."

"You don't have much privacy, then," I say.

"Oh, it's all right," he tells me. And then, with much ado, he fetches the secret relic from its niche; it's encased in plastic, rather like one of those souvenir key chains they sell outside the Vatican.

I look at it. Inside the plastic, there's a small round speck, black and shiny, rather like a polished fragment of haematite. I look but don't touch.

"Go on," he tells me, "feel it in your hand."

I take it. "Feel the surge of power," he tells me. "I know you can."

His face is earnest and full of compassion and hope. I grasp it in both hands. Is there an electric charge, a certain radiant warmth? I am not sure. There is something, I'll swear to it, but is it what the Psychic says it is? I wonder whether I have manufactured this warmth out of the young monk's enthusiasm, his obvious fervor ... or whether it is something objectively real.

But then again, having lived in the Hall of Mirrors for almost two weeks, I should know better than to believe in Objective Reality.

In the afternoon, I take a quick break to help my mother with her computer, which is having some problems. The car comes from the house to fetch me. Nothing could be more mundane than that, and yet the experience of visiting my own home is oddly jarring.

It is very strange to enter the house in these saffron robes. Everything feels different, even the way the housekeeper keeps her distance and offers me a cup of coffee with the utmost deference, placing it upon the yellow cloth I keep for receiving the offerings of women, who may not place an object directly into my hands.

One feels that a monk should visit sick and dying humans — not a sick computer. On the other hand, computers these days do have a rudimentary consciousness, and monks should not refuse any reasonable requests. I know no mantra to salve the laptop's turmoil, but it does seem to respond to my monkly cajoling.

At length, after fixing my mother's computer, I go upstairs to my room, which is on the fifth floor, up many flights of stairs in this skinny Sukhumvit townhouse.  It is not really my room, of course, because the place I call home is ten thousand miles across the ocean, but it is where I stay when I'm in Thailand, and it houses a few familiar objects, including the laptop I have carried with me from Los Angeles.

I have not checked email for twelve days, and I do so now.  There are literally hundreds of messages. Of course, few people knew that I have been in a monastery, or even that I left the United States; there are requests to go to meetings, junk mail, jokes, invoices, and quick notes and comments from friends; it occurs to me that when I come back from the monastery, my entire odyssey will be barely a glitch in the timeline, a brief delay in a response to an email, a late bill.  I do not need to tell a soul that I have been on this epic quest through inner space and time.  Momentous things have been happening, but I alone have changed; the world has not, will not.

And that, too, is an important lesson I must learn.  I am not the world.  The world is not me.  It is something we chant in chapel almost every day: these things are not of us, they are not us: let them go.

That evening, in fact, we chant it again.

Evening chapel is a breeze, for some reason. It just rushes by. Today, the Tall Pale Monk is the most senior, and he is the one who ends up chanting the leading verses. Because he seldom does it, he makes an extra effort, and his voice is soft and mellifluous against the whisper of electric fans.

Evening ... I realize that in order to leave this monastery, I must memorize another set of ancient Pali formulae.

What if I get it wrong, and accidentally ask to be ordained for life?

The Psychic monk volunteers to look up the phrases in the Big Book and to give me a transcription.

Meanwhile, I have finished composing my sermon, so tonight I will go through it and polish the words a little, since the Seer insists that the sermon should be printed in Thai and English and distributed as a little booklet.

Evening meditation: agony in that my legs became completely numb! And yet, all at once, what a strange feeling of release.

Again, as this morning, the inner stillness swoops down upon me, sudden, as uncompromising as the final cadence of a Mozart sonata. I feel myself settling, like the floorboards of an ancient house. I realize that I have never been entirely at peace before. It is so unfamiliar a sensation that I am not quite able to handle it....

And tomorrow I must learn what one has to say to the abbot in order to win release from this monastery.

*Day Thirteen*
# Music of the Night

Day Thirteen begins with a very strange, exhilarating, terrifying dream after meditating myself to sleep. I am possessed by Tomm ... yes, Sharon's Tomm ... who did, after all, tell me he would come to me in the temple. I'm uttering words of oracular wisdom in a huge temple — or is an alien spacecraft? It is certainly an alien force that possesses my body. My limbs are not my own. I orate in a powerful and resonant voice, as though I were a living trumpet. I am almost certain that I have tentacles or other protuberances, and that I can fly, slither, spin like a top. When I wake up, I am dizzy from all that spinning. It is 4:45 a.m., far too early for going out to beg for food, and the world is still completely dark.

And then it happens.

First the light. The room is flooded with it. The light is white — and cool, not blinding, not assailing my eyes. It is an all-enveloping, pure light.

Then a bizarre, buzzing, shrieking noise, as though a monstrous starship were passing overhead. I'm jolted out of my bed, sit straight up. Nothing now but the pre-dawn sounds of the temple: the stray dogs, the swish of stiff brooms on paving stones. I sit up for a moment. I am wide awake. That sound was loud enough to wake the entire temple: why aren't there hounds howling, cats mewling, cocks crowing?

Then the sound comes once again. It is a chord that slowly builds and builds, seeming to hover in the very air. It's spine-chilling. It has a brassy, almost electronic edge to it, and it seems to contain every single note in the musical spectrum, and yet I hear it as harmonious — as an exquisite, delicate, transcendental harmony — a universal harmony constrained, forged, exploding out of universal discord — out of an energy as powerful as the forces that bind the interior of an atomic nucleus, as cosmic as the curvature of space-time.

Why isn't everyone running out of the *kuti* to gaze at some divine manifestation descending from the sky?

I realize that I am the only one who is hearing this music.

The ancients, who believed that all the planets circumnavigated our anthropocentric earth on crystal spheres, believed that the grinding of these spheres in the firmament produced a music so ethereal that mere humans could not hear it.

Is this what I am listening to?

I don't have time to figure it out, because as suddenly as it begins, the music ends, leaving in the air a kind of aural after-image, whisper that hangs in the air.

Am I dreaming?

But no. I am definitely wide awake. I tell myself, I will set my alarm, I will go back to sleep for 45 minutes, and if I still remember it when I wake up, if it doesn't fade away as dreams do, I will make a note of it. And I go back to sleep, but I am charged with a strange, wild energy.

Was this an aural hallucination? Or did I touch the shadow of something huge and mystical, did I, along with mystics and mescaline addicts the world over, have an encounter with the face of God? I do not know.

But now, weeks later, going through these journal notes I made in the monastery, I still remember the chord that should have been a discord vividly.

The dream of being alien: now that, on the other hand, that is fading, is definitely part of the substance of the unconscious. And I remember that I told people (I cannot remember whom) things I could not possibly have known, and that it felt really bizarre to have lost complete control of one's body.

The odd thing is, I thought I had already received what I could receive from this leg of my inward journey; but it seems there are yet riches to be plundered.

S.P. Somtow · *Nirvana Express*

It is now 7 am, and I have gone out begging already, and had a quick breakfast with the Seer, who it seems has a perfect recollection of all my relatives, and inquires after them all.

My sermon has been written. I decided that as I know little of the arcana of Buddhism, I will write about what I do know, and I've done a little piece about the story of Phra Wetsandorn, the great compassionate figure of Buddhist mythology who was willing to give up even his own child, the thing he most loved, for the sake of the *dhamma*. It is a story that every Thai child knows, but my sermon is about a comparison of that story with that of Abraham and Isaac, a story equally familiar to Christians, Jews, and Muslims as it is in their sacred literature. I used the story to point out some differences between the world-view Buddhism and the great theistic religions of the "people of the book."

Well, my mother reads to me her translation of my sermon, and towards the end she finds herself weeping.

It is only after she has departed that I come to understand what the sermon means to me, and why I have chosen this subject, and what particular lesson it has to teach me. I have recently let go of someone I loved very deeply. But I had never let go of the love itself. It tormented me. It perhaps had a role in causing me to hear the voice in the hills of California, in driving me to this monastery.

But the sermon is teaching me that even that love must be let go. There is nothing I can do. In the end, that is undoubtedly why I came here. This is undoubtedly a major revelation for me. It explains everything. I acknowledge the fact that this love has blinded me and imperiled me, and now I let it go, I set it afloat, downriver, towards the infinite sea.

Today, the Psychic has hand-written for me the formulas for blessing the congregation after the sermon, and for asking leave of the abbot to end my inward journey.

For the journey must end soon.

I think there are a few more revelations yet, but we shall see how and when they arrive.

This afternoon, a moving visit with an 85-year-old woman who used to be the cook at my parents' house when we lived in Holland, then later in Japan.

She has come from the hospital and can hardly walk. Seeing the yellow robe, she can barely contain herself.

She weeps copiously. She weeps from the moment I enter the room and doesn't stop until I leave. I remember everything about Samphao, this woman: in Holland, I used to take her to the opera and she was the only person in the house willing to go with me. I remember her weeping over

Rigoletto's tragedy, his hump, the murder of his daughter; and I cannot help thinking about how sad she is now. It is almost as though she has become a character in one of the operas I saw with her as a teenager.

In Japan, in a zealous bit of cooking, she accidentally chopped off a little bit of her own finger. I remember the upheaval and how she wailed in pain. I wonder what she remembers; it was so long ago; I was in my teens. Seeing her weep reminds me of the bitter wind on the Scheveningen pier.

I do not know if they are tears of joy or sadness.

The sermon is now being xeroxed. Too late — there are some typos, I've found, but we can always fix it in the second printing....

In evening chapel, the novices have to chant at great length because it is what everyone calls *"wan kon"* which seems to mean "shaving day". And yet, I don't see anyone getting their head shaved! The novices chant searingly out of tune with each other, and end up in perfect thirds, thus creating an accidentally very western harmony. I get the idea that I will use such an accidental harmony in my next opera, which is going to have a seen where the chanting of monks and novices is heard in the distance, off-stage.

So I'm sitting in the painful *phabphieb* position in the chapel with the chanting reverberating around me, and I'm already composing, already thinking of the next stage in my life. That is how I know that this leg of the trip will soon be over. I wonder if it's against the 227 precepts to compose operas in chapel. It certainly is against them to go to an opera.

An astonishingly painful session with meditation, but one of the novices is having as bad a time as me, and suddenly I notice that he, too, has his eyes open; he and I are alone in this.

We start making faces at each other. A little giggle escapes his lips.

You see, Buddhism isn't all about people sitting around endlessly moping about the inevitability of karma. It is a very joyful philosophy, one that allows a measure of joy even in moments of grief, pain, and terror.

In the evening, the Seer tells me that I have indeed achieved much of what I came here to do. He says, "The world outside doesn't allow for inward journeys. This is what you have really needed, all these years, in America."

# Compassion:
## *Two Perspectives*

*a sermon by*
*Phra Yanavamso*
*(S.P. Somtow)*

*Sunday, 19 August 2001*
*Wat Somanasvihara*

I come before you today not as a learned teacher, and not one who has spent years of his life acquiring esoteric facts about Buddhism. I am not an expert on the fine points of the *dhamma*. Today I will not be enumerating for you the four states of *brahmavihara* or the five types of *piti*. In fact, I will not be using many erudite Pali words at all. One cannot preach what one does not know.

I come to you as one who has only just set out on a journey. I am perhaps only two steps ahead of you. I am feeling my way, step by step. I cannot tell you how long the journey will last, nor what we shall find at its end. But I can share with you the fleeting glimpses of the truth I have been able to learn in the past two weeks.

What I say today may sound very different from what you are used to hearing in this place. There may be a million pathways to the same truth; the road I took to get here was not the usual one. I have not read the same books, seen the same plays, or listened to the same songs as most who have preached in this venerable hall. Please do not be offended if the stories I tell are unfamiliar.

A very short time after Lord Buddha walked the earth, there lived in ancient Greece a philosopher named Socrates. Socrates was famous for answering every question with another question. It can fairly be said that his way of thought revolutionized Western civilization.

There was also in ancient Greece a very famous oracle in the town of Delphi, halfway up Mount Parnassus, the abode of the god Apollo, patron of truth. The oracle was reputed to be able to answer any question. One day, a delegation went to Delphi to ask the oracle, "Who is the wisest man alive?" The oracle answered, "Socrates."

When Socrates was told of this, he is reputed to have said, "If that is true, it's because I'm the only man in the world who knows that he doesn't know anything."

Today,  for the next thirty minutes, I am that man.  I begin by confessing my utter and unfathomable ignorance.  I can only hope that in my ignorance, I will be able to point you vaguely in the direction of wisdom.

How I came to be here today has been something of a miraculous experience.  It was only a few weeks ago, driving through the hills of California, that an inner voice impelled me to come to Bangkok and begin an inward journey.  Although my time here at the monastery is very short — it will end in a matter of days — I do not believe that the inward journey will end when I have doffed these saffron robes.

Before the coming of the inner voice, it was as though I stood in the center of a raging tempest. Great things were happening in my life — great achievements were on the horizon — and there was also churning turmoil and disenchantment.  I have an old friend, a sort of modern-day *rishi* (or hermit) who sits in a cottage atop a mountain in Georgia. She is connected to the outside world both psychically and by means of the internet.  For months, she has been telling me, she has seen a vision in which I am standing beside a lotus. Gradually, she has told me, the lotus has come closer and closer, until in her latest visions I am holding the lotus in my hand.  She is completely unfamiliar with Buddhism.  I told her that the lotus is a Buddhist symbol.  But I no idea that the vision would come literally true, and that I would finally be standing in the chapel of this temple clasping a bundle of three lotuses.

I arrived in Bangkok without a clue as to what becoming a monk might entail, only with the burning desire to begin the journey. My ignorance, you see, protected me. Had I known, for instance, that I would have to memorize several pages of ancient Pali text in order to gain entrance to this world, I might have fled in terror. As I struggled to learn those words, working from an English-language guide because my ability to read the Thai language is fairly rudimentary, I despaired.

But in the very early morning before my ordination, there came a dream of astonishing clarity and vividness. In the dream, I was standing inside a temple. The hall was suffused with a soft radiance. I watched while a coffin was being exhumed. The lid was open, and there was a rotting corpse within. Someone was stripping off the flesh, and presently there was only a skeleton left. I heard a voice: "It's ready to be cremated now." The bones were cast on a heap on the ground, just beyond the threshold.

In the dream, I walked out of the temple and trod right on top of the pile of bones, and I heard a thigh-bone cracking. I stopped. I thought: "This is disrespectful. How could I be so callous as to have stepped on the dead?" And then there came a voice once more: "These are nothing but old bones. They are empty. They are nothing. Don't think of them anymore."

When I awoke, I had lost my fear.

I did not know then that the dream of the bones was also an important lesson in the *dhamma*. Although Buddhism teaches many things, the lesson of how to *let go* is perhaps the ultimate lesson. My dream told me that in order to begin this inward journey, I had to cremate the past — not only the emotional turbulence, not only the fears and failures, but even the good things, the successes.

Although the subject of this sermon is the nature of compassion, the subject of *letting go* can never be far out of sight. The two are closely linked, and *letting go* is at the very heart of the *dhamma*.

I said that I was going to quote from different sources in order to arrive at the same destination, so let me begin by quoting from a person who never existed: the sage Obi-Wan Kenobi in *Star Wars,* who tells the young Luke Skywalker, "There is a single force that connects everything in the universe."

It is very interesting that this quintessentially Buddhist thought should be the underlying philosophy of the most influential artifact of popular culture of the last fifty years. We have reached an age, you see, when the Western world is finally ready to embrace the *dhamma*. Partly it is because of growing dissatisfaction with traditional belief systems in the West. Partly it is because of the transcendence of science as the West's prevailing mode of thought. As the twentieth century progressed, Western science has come closer and closer to Buddhism, and we shall be amazed to discover that a lot of the most revolutionary concepts of contemporary science have been foreshadowed in the teachings of the Enlightened One.

In the Western world, science has frequently taken the place of religion as the method by which to seek answers to the fundamental questions of existence. Every religion must have a mythology, and for science that mythology is science fiction. We do not have to believe that events in mythology literally occurred in order to understand that mythology illuminates profound truths. It illuminates them through the language of metaphor.

We can choose to view *Star Wars* as a rollicking adventure story, but when we see it in mythological terms, it is also the story of everyman, ourselves, questing for the nature of reality, and finally achieving victory by understanding the Self.

Our hero begins his journey just as you and I have begun ours: as a simple youth untouched by the evils of the world. He soon embarks on a war against an evil empire, using the physical weapons the human imagination has created: lasers, light sabers. But these external objects prove useless against the ultimate enemy.

And so, at the climax of the film, the inner voice of the deceased Achariya says to Luke Skywalker, "Use the force, Luke," and our hero closes his eyes. He *lets go* of his conscious self. He no longer sees with his external senses, but reaches out with his inner understanding of the universe; what he does can only be described as the result of a *vipassana* meditation. That final force of darkness that Luke vanquishes through his meditation is appropriately named the Death Star.

Appropriate, you see, because we are all trying to vanquish our personal Death Star. There are things which as human beings we all fear, and which we spend most of our lives trying to resist. The Death Star which we are trying to overcome can be described as death itself, and the forms of suffering that precede it — illness, old age, and pain. It is our desire to overcome death that has led to much of humanity's most glorious achievements: its monuments, its poetry, its great art. And yet, Buddhism and science — and our own inner voices — tell us that even these grandest of human endeavors must finally pass.

In the 6th Century B.C., about the same time as the Lord Buddha walked the earth, there lived on the island of Lesbos (today in Greece) a great poetess named Sappho. Her poetry was so widely regarded in the ancient world that every educated person knew most of her poems by heart. Her lyrics were quoted by everyone, so that one only had to utter a few words before someone else would be able to finish the poem.

Because Sappho's poetry was so well known, the papyri on which it was written were held in little regard. They were everywhere. They meant nothing. They were treated like yesterday's newspaper — good for nothing but wrapping fish. Because no one saw the value of preserving those papyri, they were cut up into strips to make the bandages used for mummifying cats in Alexandria, which was a Greek-speaking city in ancient Egypt. It was far more important to wrap dead cats than to preserve that which everybody knew.

The centuries passed, and those mummy wrappings were all that remained of the greatest lyric poet of her time. Today, what we know of Sappho's work comes from painfully unwinding the wrappings from those two-thousand-year-old cat mummies. We take a word here, a word there, and we try to piece them together into a poem. We can glimpse but the merest shadow of her greatness.

And that's after two thousand years. Who will speak of Sappho in ten thousand years, a million years?

It is human to hate and fear the fact that there is no immortality. But in order to be fully at peace, we must finally come to terms with that fact. We must finally *let go* of this ultimate terror. The road toward this *letting go* has been given to us in the form of the Dhamma.

The inevitability of cessation, in science, is known as the law of Entropy. The Third Law of Thermodynamics, the study of heat and energy, states that "Entropy must always increase to the maximum." This is just another way of stating one of essential truths of Buddhism: that the human condition is heir to suffering and death, and that if we try to fight a war against Entropy, we cannot win.

   In this sermon, I will argue that whereas
Buddhism has numerous superficial similarities to
other belief systems in the world, there is a
fundamental difference that places Buddhism closer
to the realm of modern science, and separates it from
the underlying principles of other religions,
particularly those of the west.  This will not be an
argument for the superiority of one system of
thought over another, nor criticism of other religions.
But people often ask, "What *is* the difference?  Is
there a difference at all?  Don't all religions simply
tell people to do good things and avoid evil things?"
Others, perhaps influenced by Karl Marx, may even
say, "Isn't religion just a way of controlling the
masses?" little realizing that the philosophy of Marx
is in itself a religion, and that when misused by
worldly governments, has often turned out to be one
of the most chilling ways of controlling the masses
ever invented.

   The nature of this difference, I will argue, is a
very simple one.  The great religions of the West are
systems to reverse the flow of Entropy.  They teach
that whether by faith, by good deeds, or by devotion,
one may attain to a state in which Entropy is
permanently held at bay — and that that state, called
by some Paradise (which is an ancient Hebrew word
for "orchard") is the state of existence most worthy
of attainment.  By contrast, Buddhism, like modern
science, accepts the reality of the Third Law of
Thermodynamics.  It is not a system designed to
reverse the flow of Entropy at all.  Rather, it is a

system for accepting, coming to terms with, and finally embracing Entropy.

It is a revolutionary way of thinking which only now, twenty five centuries later, scientific thought has begun to catch up with.

Just how revolutionary was Buddhism in its time? Recently I had the privilege of reading the *Dhammapada*, a collection of the Buddha's sayings. In composing a symphonic work to honor the life of the father of Thailand's modern democracy, Pridi Banomyong, I wanted to find a text that could be sung by the chorus in the work's finale. I found many of those words in the final chapter of the *Dhammapada*, in which the Buddha speaks of the kind of man he would consider a Brahmana.

The ancient biographers speak of earthquakes and blinding light and other magical portents accompanying the preaching of the Lord Buddha. But in truth, such metaphors are unnecessary. The words themselves are like earthquakes, like blinding light, tearing asunder the most cherished beliefs of their time.

One must understand that in the Sixth Century B.C., the caste system was firmly entrenched in the fabric of Indian society. To be born into the Brahmana caste made one automatically superior to other people. People's roles in the world were predetermined by their birth, and the system was so deeply ingrained as to be considered an unalterable reality of the human condition.

What we read in the final chapter of the *Dhammapada* is that the Lord Buddha completely rejects the notion that the high status of brahmana-hood is an accident of birth. Instead, he gives us a list of noble qualities — freedom from anger and vindictiveness, for example, and detachment from desire — and he follows each noble quality with the resounding refrain: "*that* one I call a brahmana." In other words, true nobility does not come from an external factor whatsoever, but only from within.

To say that such a point of view is subversive is an understatement. For the whole of human civilization is organized according to that which is external: money, power, birth, position, talent. Yet the Buddha's answer to the ultimate questions of the universe is always: *Look inside yourself.*

It is this that leads me to the topic at hand: the nature of compassion.

Compassion is a central theme of Buddhism, yet it is strangely neglected in other systems of belief. I am not sure of this, but I do not recall seeing the word at all, for instance, in the King James translation of the Bible. There is, however, another word that is prominently featured in Christian scripture, and that word is *love*. I will argue that while those two words are very close in meaning, and often go together in practice, it is, in the end, the difference between these two words that also separates the Buddhist world-view from that of Western religions.

I would like to compare two great stories, a Buddhist story and a Judaeo-Christian story, in order to demonstrate this difference.

The story of Phra Wetsandorn, the last of the Jataka tales, is so familiar to Thais that it does not bear repeating. It is the story of the final incarnation before the Great Being was to come back to earth as the Enlightened One. Whether or not one takes the Jataka tales literally, they are important in that each one illuminates one the qualities necessary to become Enlightened.

Very briefly summarized, the story of Phra Wetsandorn is about a prince so generous of heart that he gives away all that he possesses. Finally, the prince is asked by the villainous Chuchok to give away what he most loves: his wife and children.

He does so. And in that moment, having overcome even that most binding of all human attachments, the love of a parent for his child, he has done the final act that allows him to be reborn as the Enlightened One.

The story has, of course, many twists and turns, and in the end the wife and children are redeemed and the villain is punished for his own greed, but these are not the essence of the story. The essence is that Phra Wetsandorn gives up his own child and thus becomes ready for Buddha-hood.

When one tells this story to people in the West, they often find it shocking, indeed immoral. What emotion, they say, could be more pure, more redemptive, than love? How could such a cruel action be a necessary prelude to Enlightenment?

To understand this, one must turn to a story that is told in the Torah, the Jewish holy book, which is also a part of the Christian bible. It is a story as familiar to Westerners as the story of Phra Wetsandorn is to the Buddhist community. It is the story of the patriarch Abraham and his son Isaac, who may have lived some five centuries before the birth of the Buddha. Thus, in terms of mythological time, Abraham and Phra Wetsandorn are contemporaries.

As the story is unfamiliar to Buddhists, perhaps I should tell it briefly.

Like Phra Wetsandorn, Abraham was a great leader of his people, much beloved, full of wisdom and generosity. In her old age, by a special blessing from God, his wife conceives a child named Isaac, who grows up to be the thing that Abraham most dearly loves.

One day, however, God tells Abraham that to prove his devotion to him, he must take Isaac up to the mountain and sacrifice him. Abraham's heart is heavy, but he must obey. He cannot bear to tell his son what is about to happen until they have almost reached the place of sacrifice.

Because of his great love for his father, Isaac understands that the sacrifice needs to take place, and he allows himself to be prepared for death without complaint. Abraham lifts up the knife and gets ready to slay his son.

At the last moment, however, an angel appears and tells Abraham that God was, well, "just kidding." "Behold," the angel says, "there's a ram over there, caught in a thicket by his horns. Sacrifice the ram instead of your son." Happy ending. Abraham never has to go through with it. He kills the ram, and they go down the mountain, praising God and full of joy.

In its major plot points, then, we have a story remarkably similar to the story of Phra Wetsandorn. The ability to sacrifice one's child is a kind of final test, a sort of Ph.D. in religious studies. But although the story is the same, the lesson we learn from it is utterly different.

The story of Abraham and Isaac is about love; the story of Phra Wetsandorn is about compassion.

In the end, the question that God poses to Abraham is a simple one: "Whom do you love more, your child or Me?" The quality of love that Abraham shows for his God is what the Hindus would call *bhakti,* which we usually translate as devotion. It is because of Abraham's love for God that he is willing to sacrifice the earthly thing that is most dear to him; and it is because of God's love for Abraham that Abraham is, as it were, let off the hook. We are to learn from this that love engenders mercy. This is certainly a profound truth, and one that Buddhists can relate to.

But in the story of Phra Wetsandorn, the defining state of mind is compassion. When the prince's son asks him why he must do what he must do, you can just hear this little boy's voice saying, as a million children have said to their parents throughout human existence, as Isaac must have said to Abraham, "Why, father?  Don't you love me?"  We must remember that nobody lets Phra Wetsandorn off the hook at the last minute.  It is not a test.  It is for real.  No angel intervenes to tell the prince that God was "just kidding."   And we must believe, because we believe that Phra Wetsandorn was endowed with the noblest virtues of a human being, that his love for his child was the equal of any other human's — that it was in fact the perfect pattern of such a love.

This is the crux of the story, because to a Western perspective, the burning question must be, "How could he possibly do this?   Doesn't he love his children?"    And the key to this dilemma is compassion.

Phra Wetsandorn tells his child that there are millions of creatures in the universe, trapped in an endless cycle of suffering.  Millions of creatures for whom he feels compassion, whose voices cry out for an end to their pain.  Because of the magnitude of his compassion, he must *let go* even that most precious of all human attachments.  It is not because he does not feel this love that he does what he does.  Indeed, it is the very vastness of his love that makes the sacrifice so complete.

The story of Phra Wetsandorn, then, despite its many similarities to that of Abraham and Isaac, is

entirely different in its purpose and in the lessons we
learn from it.

It is human nature to create Gods that are mirror
images of ourselves. The God of Love is perhaps the
noblest creation of Western civilization. Because
love in the pure sense is the most powerful of human
feelings, it is human nature to feel that a God who is
defined as Love should be the most powerful way of
reversing the flow of Entropy. We are so much in
love with Love that it is natural for us to want to
believe that Love is eternal. How many thousands of
lifetimes it must have taken for the Bodhisatta to
reach the stage where he could see beyond love!

But the *dhamma* teaches us that in the end, even
love itself must pass. We will inevitably be parted
from everything we love. Entropy can be reversed
only for a short time.

It is compassion that allowed the Bodhisatta to
accept, and finally let go, of love itself.

And yet compassion is far more difficult to
understand than love. Love is instinctive. An infant
is born loving the mother as she holds it in her arms.
We do not need to be taught love. But the ability to
feel the suffering of others is another matter. It is
something that must be learned, slowly, throughout
one's life. To learn to feel compassion for all the
sentient creatures of the universe must surely take
many lifetimes.

Please do not think that I am asking you not to
love. Love is a gift we are all born with. But to grow
in compassion is not to diminish love. We may start

by feeling compassion for those we love; but we should continue, each day of our lives, to try to feel for those we do not love, those to whom we are indifferent, and even those we hate. If we cannot extend our compassion throughout the entire universe, at least we must try to do so little by little, even one soul at a time.

For every time that we learn to feel compassion for any creature, however insignificant, we are also advancing, step by step, towards the one truth that Buddhism holds eternal, the *dhamma*.

As I have said, I do not come before you as a great teacher of the dhamma, but to share with you a few brief moments of insight I have had in my short time in this monastery. In three days I will return to the outside world. I do not know whether I will even have mastered the art of putting on these robes by the time I leave. Having spent my entire life as one of the smartest kids in the class, it is uniquely humbling to find myself suddenly the stupidest. But as I stand here with you, at the very beginning of this new journey, I can already tell you that I have discovered a serenity, an inner peace, that I never thought I would find.

May my words awaken in all of you today the desire to seek the path of wisdom, the strength to be truly compassionate, and the courage to let go.

*Day Fourteen*
# Pure At Last

Today would have been the last full day of my monkhood if we had followed the schedule originally planned. But astrology has reared its ugly head; the Seer tells me that Day 15 will not be appropriate, and then a Prophesying Nun has told my sister that the day after Day 15 won't be appropriate either, putting my whole family into a state of panic. Finally, a compromise is reached, and the Prophesying Nun is satisfied if I leave after 18 days, as long as I remain within the confines of the Temple until 11 a.m.

Otherwise, she tells my sister, it will mean doom.

I have always viewed the various Prophesying Nuns and Seers that orbit about Bangkok's spirit-filled society with some skepticism. This particular Nun has always advised me to give food to monks in order to improve my lot in life — and giving food to monks is itself a wonderful thing to do, regardless of whether one wants to improve one's lot in life or not — but she always specifies the exact kinds of food that must be given, and the colors of the plastic bags in which the food must be delivered to the monks. That I always found a little weird.

I once asked my sister to ask this Prophesying Nun directly — why the colored bags?

"Oh," the nun told her, "they are color-coded — they are karmic luggage tags — directing the flow of your karma to the, as it were, correct airport of destiny."

How can one argue against such relentless logic?

This major day dawns with my mother appearing at the gates of the temple as I emerge with my begging bowl. A lot of snapshots are taken as she inserts a bag of rice and pork into my bowl.

Not only is this a day of my sermon, but it's also a day of Patimokha, the day in which the monks gather to hear the entire monk's code recited ... all 227 rules. I am dreading the sitting, dreading it all. I know that I will have to sit in a very bizarre position, on a special sermonizing throne, for the duration of the entire sermon. Then, of course, there will be the Patimokha, and, depending on the reciting monk's mnemonic skills, that could last anything from forty-five minutes to an hour and a half.

This day should be the climax of everything, yet I'm filled with a nagging dread — could it be stage fright? I haven't felt this kind of stage fright in a very long while.

A photo-op in the morning for the entire "school year" of monks. The Guru himself descends from the celestial wooden *kuti*, turns movie director, fussing over the exact stance and posture of each monk, the placement of the hands, and so on; then he gets a few solo pictures taken; "after all," he says, "some of you might like my picture as a souvenir." Presently he wanders off alone with the photographer. Has he been nurturing a secret desire to be a Playgirl centerfold, I wonder to myself? Soon he can be seen in the distance, posing next to various picturesque sacred objects, trees, statuary, what have you. Nothing ostentatious, mind you, and always the beatific smile of one who has glimpsed Nirvana.

At 9:30, being a *wan phra,* there's a sermon in the main vihara; an aged monk recites from a banana-leaf scroll book as dozens of monks, nuns, and laypersons sit in various positions of contorted discomfort. Our presence as new monks is required. We seat ourselves on the monks' dais, all of us, wearing our robes in the special *wan phra* style — oh yes, did I not explain there is a THIRD style of wearing the robes, in which a second robe, folded, is draped over one shoulder and dangles down almost to the ground? This second robe is the *sangkati*, and I am not entirely sure why one must wear it on these High Holy Days, but it certainly lends an added dash of flamboyance to one's couture.  Especially since my *sangkati* doesn't match my regular robe. The regular robe has been washed a few times by now; the *sangkati* is virgin, straight from the package, its color still vibrant.  This two-tone effect is not intentional, but I see that most of the monks have it. In fact, during the photo-op earlier, the Guru has been at great pains to have us all trade our *sangkatis* back and forth to find the closest color coordination.

The sight of row upon row of monks, beneath the towering and motionless golden Buddha, on whom a dozen life-sized Bodhisattas gaze in perpetual adoration, is curiously stirring.  The ancient monk drones on; his speech is accompanied by the ostinato knell of grandfather clocks, none of which keeps the same time as any other. The sermon is one that has been preached a thousand times in this very room.  Every word has the weight of time. I feel the words as they fall from the monk's lips, clinging to our robes, to the columns with their fading frescoes of the Buddha's lives, wafting on threads of incense.

My sermon, I know, will be a lot different, for it is as virginal as my *sangkati*.  It begins by examining the question of why, at the end of *Star Wars*, Luke Skywalker uses what is clearly a *vipassana* meditation technique in order to destroy the Death Star.  It talks about east and west, and about the difference between love and compassion — which in a nutshell is also the difference between Buddhism and the western religions. There's also a long comparison between the story of Phra Wetsandorn and that of Abraham and Isaac.

So this is the strange thing. At 2 p.m., I enter the small hall which has been set aside for my sermon. The press, for some reason, has been alerted, and as I sit, quietly preparing myself, I suddenly find myself giving an interview to a T.V. station. It appears that the outside world has infiltrated my inner journey — big time. And yet I don't mind. I'm returning to that world soon enough. It's good to be reminded.

But, midway through the sermon, I suddenly realize that I have not composed these words in order to instruct this audience on the intricacies of Buddhism — after all, what can I possibly know of these things after only a few weeks in a monastery? The words are aimed not at them after all, but at myself. The lessons about love — about loving too much — and about redemption by letting go — are things that I badly needed to learn, advice I never heeded; indeed, the voice that utters these words to me, I see now, is the same inner voice that plucked me from a California freeway and plunked me down inside this pocket universe.

This epiphany is so overwhelming that I begin to weep, copiously and unabashedly, as I preach the last pages of the sermon. It does not matter that there are television cameras in my face, and that the sermon will, as I will soon discover, appear on

national cable that very night ... that's all external
stuff. What matters is that I've reached, well, not the
end of the inward journey of course, for that is a
journey I now know will never end, but at least a
way station, a rest stop, if you will, since the freeway
metaphor seems to run through this whole thread of
my life.

What does this mean?   That the sermon was
created merely to cleanse my own grief, and not to
help others?   Is this some kind of narcissistic,
solipsistic fantasy I'm living in? I do not know.

But before I know it, the sermon is over, and I
have made my way through the whole thing without
ever suffering a single spasm in my poor arthritic
knees.  In fact, I feel no pain at all.  It is as if the
physical pain had been merely a projection of an
inner torment, and in a sense, I no longer need it.

At five o'clock comes a confessional; we monks
all kneel before one another, wherever we may be,
and   confess   all   our   infractions   of   the   227
commandments of monkhood.  We don't actually
confess every single peccadillo; rather, there are
ritual Pali phrases that seem to cover the main
classes of offense, and other phrases that grant
absolution.   And then there are sort of blanket
phrases for any class of offense one might have
actually left off the list.

This is very useful as one never knows if one has
accidentally stepped on an ant, or thoughtlessly
urinated while standing up — all these things are
strictly *verboten*.

The Patimokkha is a ceremony that monks must by no means miss. The text itself provides very, very specific circumstances in which a Patimokkha recital may be interrupted. For example, one is allowed to desist from the recital if a tiger or snake happens to enter the chapel. The text also explains that if a king happens to pass through, the monks may cease their recital in order to greet him, though they must continue afterwards from where they left off.

I am not sure why the 227 precepts must be recited from memory, or even why some of them are several pages long, with as many sections and subsections as a typical clause in the American Internal Revenue Service regulations. Everyone tells me that the pain will be good for one, purifying and ennobling, not unlike listening to the complete Bartok string quartets whilst lying on a bed of nails.

To my amazement, however, the Patimokkha is not an ordeal at all. Perhaps I am still buoyed up by the experience in the sermon. But for one thing, the reciting monk fairly whips through the entire thing. If I were not following it word for word in my transliteration/translation, I would surely not believe that a human being could memorize a couple of hundred pages of an alien text so perfectly and utter it so fast. I have the advantage of knowing what it all means — my fellow monks do not have the translation in front of them. It is a sublime experience, and I emerge from it feeling reborn.

Tonight will be my farewell to the Guru, my Abbot. I finally meet up with him in his rooms,

which are in a wooden stilted building, very
traditional, far in the back of the temple; the Seer,
because of his astrological fame, has received many
endowments from happy "customers" and lives in
relative luxury compared to the Abbot. Indeed, I've
been fortunate in lodging in the Seer's *kuti,* which
even had air conditioning.

The Abbot is suprisingly gentle this evening.
Well, relatively gentle; he orders me to fold my
palms, and barks out a blessing. I feel a bit like
when I was 17 and leaving Eton, and, as all boys
leaving school, had a private interview with
Anthony Chenevix-Trench — notorious for beating
children while drunk, though I never experienced
this myself.

The Abbot's blessing seems a bit perfunctory, but
then again he does have a 4 a.m. plane to catch, and
will be teaching the monastic virtues to new monks
in the South of Thailand. I leave his rooms with a
strangely ambivalent feeling. But that doesn't last.
When I reach the narrow pathway that leads back to
my lodging, I am seduced again by the fragrance of
the night and the remarkable sense of calm.

Soon I'll be expelled from paradise all over again,
but for the moment I am suffused with happiness
and peace.

# 227 Commandments

The Judaeo-Christian world has ten commandments. Many of them are only four words long: *Thou shalt not steal.* Some are a little bit wordier. This one, for instance: "You shall not covet your neighbor's house. You shall not covet your neighbor's wife, or his male or female servant, his ox or donkey, or anything that belongs to your neighbor." One wonders why donkeys are singled out when there's also "anything else belonging to your neighbor" thrown in in case Moses missed something. Of course, there were a few problems getting too many words onto a couple of stone tablets, so one can be forgiven for the terseness.

Buddhism offers a mere five for laypersons, and they are mostly couched in positive terms rather than forbidding people to do things.

The first precept is the "thou shalt not kill" one, and it too is only four words long, but in the Pali language a word can carry a lot more meaning: *"Pāṇātipātā veramaṇī sikkhāpadaṃ samādiyāmi."* This means basically "I undertake the training precept of refraining from onslaught on breathing beings." In other words, don't harm living creatures, though plants seem to be exempt.

The other four are similar in tone — I undertake not to take anything that is not given — to indulge in misconduct over sensual pleasures — to abstain from alcohol or drugs that may cause me to lose mindfulness — to abstain from false truths.

There's one that's missing from the Ten Commandments: overindulgence in intoxicating substances — and six that are missing from the Buddhist commandments: graven images, honouring one's parents, no other gods apart from G-d, keeping the Sabbath, covetousness, and swearing.

Adultery and false witness are a grey area, since the equivalent Buddhist commandments are actually a lot more wide-ranging. They are also a lot less specific, because they are promises to abstain, not acknowledgments that there are rules that can't be broken.

Thus, "religion" puts far fewer restrictions on the average Buddhist; indeed they are not restrictions per se but more like recommendations ... following the precepts will push your karma into positive areas, but it is important to understand that *baap,* the general word for doing immoral things, is not the same as "sin" which is specifically *not* a Buddhist idea. Buddhism doesn't deal with crime and punishment, but with cause and effect.

Okay, so five commandments seem okay; novice monks have to follow an extra three and nuns have ten, the additional ones mostly being not unlike vows of poverty ("not sleeping in a high comfortable place," "not touching money" and so on.)

And then there's a quantum leap, because monks have to follow 227 precepts.

And some of them are *very* wordy, with lots of subsections, like a legal text.

Some of the more bizarre ones: "I will not defecate or urinate while standing." and of course the infamous "When a bhikkhu is having a large dwelling built, he may supervise two or three layers of facing to plaster the area around the window frame and reinforce the area around the door frame the width of the door opening, while standing where there are no crops to speak of. Should he supervise more than that, even if standing where there are no crops to speak of, it is to be confessed."

There's also a preamble to the rules which states the rules for reading the rules; I already mentioned that the recital of the rules may not be interrupted except under a number of carefully enumerated circumstances, such as a tiger wandering into the hall, a king dropping in, and so on.

All these rules together are known as the *Patimokkha* and twice a month, all the monks gather to hear someone recite the entire thing, in the Pali language, *from memory.* And because we must all be pure before hearing this recital, we go through a confession and purifying ritual, much like the idea of dropping in on the confessional before taking communion.

It is a matter if great pride to have the ability to recite the entire *Patimokkha* from memory, and a great honour to be selected to do the recital. But while we are all seated on the floor, palms held together and linked in a great spiral chain, I'm the only person in the monastery who has a crib. I'm following the recital with a Pali transliteration and English translation, and therefore am the only one bemused by some of these rules, which really do seem to come from an ancient time.

And the other thing is the *speed.*

Recital of this entire thing, in an ancient language with all its sections and subsections, takes about forty minutes thanks to the fact that the recitation is very much high-speed. As I look around, I can see that no one understands a word of it. Only I do, with the cheat sheet in my hand.

And on some level, I do feel that I'm cheating, that somehow the experience is improved by not understanding it....

*Day Fifteen*

# A Kind of Death

Day Fifteen begins with an appalling mess.  I wake up feeling very sick.  My throat is on fire.  Time is short.  I go downstairs and my begging bowl is crawling with ants; I cannot wash it without killing some, so I have to ask the Seer's assistant to help me. When I leave the temple I find I have left my shoes on, and I must leave them at a nearby noodle stand. Crossing the street, one of the well-wishers tells me I have my robe on wrong, and another monk helps me with it; then, on the way back, picking up my shoes, the lid falls off the begging bowl.   I have a severe sore throat as well, and a slight temperature.

On my return, I'm told that if the lid falls off, it entails seven days of chanting.  I've never heard this before and frankly, it worries me. It seems an ill-omened morning after the extraordinarily beautiful day yesterday. I think it is here to remind me that the world beyond is still there, and that soon I will be setting forth once more on that perilous journey back to the outside.

After breakfast I feel so ill that I don't make it to the morning chapel, but concerned monks drop by my chamber and fuss, and the Psychic finally brings me some traditional Thai medicines.

It is perfectly clear that the time has come to leave the monastery. At the *chan pen* or pre-noon meal, my sister shows up and tells me that my sermon was on the evening news — as a main headline. "Somtow preaches in the temple for the first and last time," runs the teaser. The news was in Thai and English. It is clear that this bubble of serenity will soon be broken because now everyone knows where I am. Is this a good thing? I wonder. I am confused.

However, the Seer tells me one good piece of news: the lid flying off does *not* entail seven days of chanting; rather, dropping the entire alms-bowl on the ground would be the occasion for a serious ritual of regeneration. I am relieved at this.

A kind of malaise settles over me. I remain in my room for hours. I believe that this is a kind of "harrowing of hell" that needs to take place, a temporary death before my resurrection as a layman, which will occur within an hour of the dawn on Wednesday.

It's a still point in the inward journey, a moment of reflection. This little sickness is a metaphor for my soul, which must take this day to heal itself, in its own time and in its own manner.

As evening comes, my room fills up with the entire corpus of my year of monks. They have come to cheer me up from my sickness. There is such a warm and loving atmosphere here.

The Psychic anoints my forehead with a traditional Thai herbal medicine and gently pushes some pressure points, making my pain fade away. We sit chatting about the outside world, and I answer questions about Los Angeles.

Then later, a tenor from the Bangkok Opera Chorus shows up to discuss music, and finally the Philosopher shows up to ask for some advice on translating his very earnest booklet about avoiding suicide.

It's been a strange day, but a fruitful one. As I go to sleep, my mother calls, telling me to remember to take my medicine....

I realize suddenly that this was to have been the final day of my monkhood. Until the intervention of the Seer and the Nun.

*Day Sixteen*

# A Slow Farewell

My last full day of monkhood begins with a nightmare about eating human flesh.

*My adopted son Johnny and I are sitting in the bleachers of what appears to be a racecourse. We are handed bowls. The human flesh exudes a fluffy, revolting greenish cotton candy-like substance that sticks to my face and causes me to wake up in horror.*

Fear remains with me for a while, and I have to sleep with the bathroom light on.

It is just after midnight. I sleep fitfully. My throat is very sore despite the amoxycillin. I am determined at this stage to do everything right today, after yesterday's debacle. Actually I feel fine except for the burning in my throat.

It may well be my last begging. One of the
faithful, once more, adjusts my clothing as I walk
through the market place. It seems quite clear now
that I will never master the art of wearing the robes.
As I am about to cross the road, a lady flags me
down and places a bunch of bananas in my bowl,
and a can of Pepsi. Somehow this can of soda
becomes for me a symbol of the outside world, the
commercial universe I must soon reenter.

The outside world does intrude, in the form of a
newspaper reporter. We have a long and very deep
conversation about the nature of Buddhism. It's
very interesting to me because I think there are
deep-rooted semantic problems in any such
discussion. No one has ever found the exact nuances
in English — and perhaps Thai as well — for those
Pali language concepts. I think that we always see
Buddhist philosophy through a kind of mirror-lens;
like the observer in quantum physics, we end up not
being separable from the observed.

It seems that two weeks is just about as long as I
can get away with, arriving in Bangkok, without the
appearance of the press.

A beautiful feast to mark my departure in the
Hall of Eighty Years; twenty-five monks, all the new
ones in my division except for the Athlete, who
unfortunately has been summoned to another
chanting. Everyone has chipped in for this feast — I
mean, all sorts of devotees have brought food to the

temple. Of course, my stay is short; most people stay for at least three months. But I could just as well have been there for years; my departure is felt by the others keenly. One of the monks says, "You're like a father to us." Of course, this is because all these young monks are only twenty years old ... I've arrived at the monastery with an unusual burden of experience.

That evening, the Psychic becomes possessed by an ancient sage. It's almost routine now, the gravelly voice, the curious tone of authority — a cross between Yoda and a Noh actor.

So even now, at the very last, I am still seeing strange and miraculous things, perhaps.

And now, it's coming up to bedtime and I'm experiencing a peculiar reluctance to learn the "exit formula" ... the magic words I must speak to become transformed from a symbol of the *dhamma* into a normal human being. It's just a few words of Pali. I suppose if I get it wrong, I won't be leaving the monkhood. And that is probably why the words simply won't stick in my head.

All night long, I lie tossing and turning. My throat aches hideously, and I keep waking up to suck on Strepsils.

*Day Seventeen*

# The Life of a Mosquito

The entry into this hidden community was marked with complex rituals. The departure is just one sentence. No, I did not succeed in learning that sentence. I did not want to let go.

But the last step in learning to let go is to let go of the letting go. I think that is why the departing formula is so abrupt, so sudden. It's like the last chord of a great symphony; after going through that whole experience, the end steals up on you.

This morning, I'm thinking about everything that I've learned, and about the one thing I have to say I mostly strongly disagree with. I mean to say when the Abbot was preaching to us about the life of a mosquito.

You recall that while we were squatting in the immense hall, trying to will ourselves into transcendental states, the Abbot told us how to kill mosquitoes without killing them.

*Leave the window open. Spray a little in the direction of the window, but don't spray the mosquito itself. If the mosquito makes a conscious choice to go out through the window, it will encounter vapors of death ... but you did not intentionally kill it ... it was the mosquito's karma, not yours.*

Almost two decades later, I still find myself reacting negatively to the Abbot's theory of involuntary manslaughter. Because I can't help thinking, no matter what I tell myself — *I really did mean to kill that mosquito.*

In Thailand, people do not put their dogs to sleep if they're suffering. That would be bad karma. They would rather leave the dog at a temple compound, and let the animal die somewhere far away. Because after all, the dog will still have a chance to live, however slim.

In Thailand, firing squads shoot from behind a curtain so that no one person can ever knowingly have taken a life.

Does karma have loopholes?

I do not think the Buddha's teaching really allowed for loopholes. Rather they have evolved over time. It's like the cheese and cough drop orgies I imagine the monks have late at night, even though we are not allowed to eat — because those foods can be defined as medicines — and consuming them might vaguely be considered therapy, not eating.

And yet — how ironclad is karma, really?

Does karma have fuzzy logic?

Because when we talk about how karma is perceived, both in religions that teach about karma, Buddhism and Hinduism, *and* in pop-culture philosophy in the west, the basic premise is "If I do something bad, I'll come back as an earthworm."

The Buddha's philosophy may be universal, but he was also a product of his time. He was born into Hinduism, and his starting point was the values of Hinduism, just as Christian thought must ultimately derive from Jewish paradigms.

The whole coming-back-as-an-earthworm was part of the world view that Prince Siddhartha was born into. And yet when you look at the essence of his philosophy, are we really going to come back as earthworms?

First, this is a philosophy in which *nothing exists*.

If you follow this logic to its conclusion, then the soul, which must extinguish itself like a candle once Nirvana is attained, is not really an *individual* thing with a separate identity. Any such identity is part of the illusion, and clinging to that which is ultimately all illusion is the basis of suffering.

If the soul that wants to kill the mosquito is an illusion, and the soul that wants to fly toward the poison gas-cloud is an illusion, then where is the murder?

When you look behind every illusion and see another illusion, and so on until the last illusion is stripped away, what do you see?

The genius of the human spirit is that these things can exist inside the theater of our minds, and simultaneously, the idea that they are not real may also exist there. The myriad multiverses of Stephen Hawking and the nul universe of the Buddha are perfectly congruent within the confines of one human skull.

In the end it is not karma that is fuzzy, but existence itself, which is a kind of fuzziness against the backdrop of perpetual nonexistence.

Does this even make sense?

Anyway, there I am, on the morning of returning to the real world, thinking the kind of cosmic thoughts that supposedly only come from partaking of forbidden substances.

Interrupting my rêverie, I go downstairs to the sitting room of the Seer. At the door, I pause. I look in. He is being naughty — he is watching a TV soap opera. That's against the *ten* precepts, let alone 227.

I slip away and walk once more around the temple grounds ... through cloister, trying to be mindful with each step and pausing every ten steps to contemplate, to breathe ...

The vihara with its fading murals ...

A step at a time ... *bud - dho - bud - dho*

And finally, I am back at the door to the Seer's sitting room. He hears me coming and reaches for the remote; the soap opera becomes a newscast.

The Seer smiles and he says to me, "Come in." And he tells me to fold my palms.

I don't remember the formula; when I was supposed to learn it, I was stressing about the nature of reality and illusion. But it turns out I didn't have to remember it.

The Seer just says, "Repeat after me," and it's a couple of very short sentences, and that's it. It's over.

And so I step back out into the real world. I can embrace my mother without polluting myself with a woman's touch. I can compose. I can dance and sing and do frivolous things; I can make love and I can eat a massive rare steak after midnight. One might easily think it is like being freed from a jail cell.

Yet I do not feel that I have been liberated.

Indeed, in some ways, it seems that I am re-entering a cage – a cage that I never knew I was in before. Because the journeys I took inside the walls of the Somanas Temple ... inside the walls of my mind ... took me to infinitely farther spaces than I've known before.

I get infinitesimally closer to understanding what it's like to be someone like Stephen Hawking: confined in the flesh, utterly free in his mind to roam the vastness of the cosmos.

There were the visions: the vistas, the strange new worlds I encountered during those hours in enforced meditation where … after a really long time … the agony was replaced by a preternatural stillness.

And most mind-blowing of all, there was the aural "vision" — hallucination — that seemed at first to be some science fiction rêverie — but now seems like the breath of the infinite *atman*.

Leaving the temple and walking slowly towards the waiting car, I do not yet know if Buddhism is "true". Indeed, I am not even sure that "truth", in any sense, exists. The question famously posed by Pontius Pilate seems so important in the Judaeo-Christian world, and so irrelevant in the context of Buddhism. The quest for *truth* is essential to all of western thought, but only Buddhism delivers the answer that it is all illusion.

Seventeen days have opened so many doors. Pandora's box contains another box, and another and another.

I've been opening those boxes ever since.

*Day Six Thousand, Five Hundred and Seventy*
# Linear and Non-linear

I wrote most of the words in this diary in the year 2001. It seems like the blink of an eye, but eighteen years have gone by. Parts of the diary appeared in *The Nation* in that same year, but much of it just stayed in my computer. As my computer was upgraded, so these files remained, hidden in plain sight.

This was not a story I set out to write. This was not a journey I intended to take.

In the last chapter of the diary, I wrote of stepping out of that hidden world and back into the bustling, noisome, quarrelsome, cacophonous world of the twenty-first century. Today, I set these words out one more time, realizing that I have never really left the monastery. In a very real sense, I am still there.

One thing that happened is that shortly after I left the monastery, the 9/11 tragedy occurred. I was a bit too nervous to fly back to Thailand right away and so I stayed behind for what I thought would just be a few months, but ended up with throwing myself into a huge new project — creating an opera company. (My opera *Madana* had premiered earlier than year, but I had thought of it as a one-off.

Opening the boxes within boxes…

I started the opera, the youth program, the new orchestras, with a great deal of optimism and enthusiasm. I didn't come to Thailand to take away anyone's slice of the pie; I came to try to make more pie for everyone. Not many people saw it this way, though, so it's been an incredible struggle.

Yet in the midst of chaos, there is this little room of calm. I didn't have that before.

The last eighteen years have been a whirlwind of creativity, and I finally came back to Buddhism as a major source of inspiration when I started composing the *DasJati* series.

This wasn't an idea that sprang full-grown into my mind; rather it evolved, in my subconscious, for many years before suddenly exploding into my awareness.

There was an Indian-American opera conductor named Viswa Subbaraman. He was working in Texas, and he received a commission to put on an opera set in India. He had one all picked out, but suddenly the rights became unavailable. Scanning the internet for some kind of opera about something Indian, he chanced upon a video of my opera

*Ayodhya,* which tells the entire story of India's epic poem, the *Ramayana,* in a single evening. To his (and my) surprise, he discovered that he was a friend of mine on Facebook — I am not sure how this happened. By the way, Facebook happened long after the events in the monastery above — if you can imagine a world without it.

So, I got a mysterious message which said, "Is there any way you can reduce the *Ayodhya* opera to a chamber work, with an orchestra of, say, fifteen?"

Now, *Ayodhya* is a huge festival work. It is scored for triple woodwind, harpsichord and Wagner tubas and six harps and a huge array of Thai instruments … so, indeed, reducing it for a fifteen piece ensemble would be very difficult indeed. So, my famous last words escaped my lips (or my fingers, since this was all being done online) "It would be easier to write a new opera."

"Done!" was the response.

It was then that my time at the monastery came to mind. The scenes from the Jataka Tales on the fading, fragmented murals in the main chapel. And a character from those tales, which are told about previous incarnations of the Buddha and which form a large body of the folklore of Buddhism, sprang unbidden into my consciousness: Temiya, the Silent Prince.

Temiya is an incarnation of the Buddha, a Bodhisattva, on his long journey towards Buddhahood. He is a prince in the magical kingdom of Varanasi (today Benares) and has a charmed childhood. On the day he comes of age, his father has a special gift for him. He will give the boy a taste of kingship.

"Here you are," he says, "here is a condemned criminal. Give the order for his execution, and feel the power and the responsibility of kingship."

As a Bodhisattva, the prince cannot take life. As a follower of the *dhamma,* he cannot disobey his father. So he responds to the traumatic choice by retreating into silence. Eventually, after years of frustrated attempts to get the prince to speak, the King of Kashi orders the boy's execution. The boy speaks only to save the executioner, his father's faithful servant, from the karmic horror of having slain a Bodhisattva.

An opera in which the main character is silent is an amazing challenge, and I had always wanted to tell this story. And in the end I did; I composed the opera, it was performed in a small theater in Houston and to my amazement, it turned out to be a full house and the first genuine *Buddhist* opera — for Richard Wagner had planned a Buddhist opera once, *Die Sieger,* about the disciples of the Buddha, but had never completed it; only a few notes remain and much of the music was subsumed into *Parsifal.*

The opera — which you can watch as a mytho-historical piece, a costume drama, or as a story about a modern family unable to cope with their "special" child — basically made me into an instant someone, and I will always value Viswa's predictive vision in believing such a work could be written. But the next things to happen were odder still.

First, we'd been having an annual choral festival in Bangkok — beginning with the idea dreamed up by some Czech friends of mine of a choir competition in Pattaya. So, with all these international choirs descending on Thailand, I'd started doing a "big work" that we couldn't normally do all by ourselves in Bangkok, expanding the event from Pattaya to Bangkok. We'd done Mahler 8, the "Symphony of a Thousand." In 2014, our plan was do the very impressive, and massive, *War Requiem* by Benjamin Britten.

At the moment, a coup struck. Now, there was a time when Thailand seemed to have a coup every October, but they had become much rarer. Terrified of news reports, most of the foreign choirs elected not to show up. I still had to do a big choir event, though, because the sponsors had already paid for it.

I reached back to the 1990s, when I'd written a symphony inspired by King Rama IX's adaptation of the *Mahajanaka Jataka,* the story of a pre-Buddha who is shipwrecked and, never losing hope, keeps swimming, until the goddess Mekhala plucks him from the ocean. It's about persistence and faith and keeping your goal always before you. So I did a quick adaptation of this work into a staged performance, added more scenes, and I had another work based on one of the ten iconic "Lives of the Buddha" — Nos. 1 and 2, to be exact.

The ten "big" jataka tales began to fascinate me more and more; not just the stories themselves which are so variegated and unpredictable, but the huge mass of ancillary commentary, the intricate lines of connection drawn to create a huge philosophical structure with ten cardinal virtues, one illustrated by each of the tales. It is a monumental achievement of Theravada Buddhism and an amazing example of persistence in itself.

The stories, you see, were never designed as one massive narrative. Some are folk tales that were woven into the collection; some were ancient when Buddha was alive, some were added long after he died. Some of them are epic, some, like children's stories, are straightforward and brief. They are bound together, sometimes almost perfunctorily, by a formula in which at the end of each tale, the Buddha explains to his followers who he was in that incarnation, and who his followers were.

I was next drawn to the story of Bhuridat, the dragon prince, which is No. 6 in the Thai version of the Ten Lives canon. (Not every Buddhist canon has the tales in the same order). And it was in the middle of this that "lightning" struck, because if I was already adapting my third "Jataka" tale, I might as well do all ten.

It's difficult to explain just how epic this lightning bolt was; perhaps I can do so better by quoting the text of a TEDx talk I gave about it....

Here goes:

*Riding the Lighting*
*a TEDx Talk by S.P. Somtow*

It's said that lightning doesn't strike the same place twice. As artists, we are told that inspiration is like lightning: we wait on a hilltop until one day the spark comes that brings with it achievements, riches, and fame.

The truth, as any pilot will tell you, is that lightning strikes the same place all the time. So do those bolts of inspiration. It's what we do with that spark that I want to talk about.

Everyone here today has at one time or another been struck with "a big idea" — one that by its very nature must change the way the world perceives reality. A "big idea" starts with "what if?" — "What if people could fly?" — "What if the earth went around the sun?" — "What if we had a play in which the words were all sung?"

For every "big idea" that springs to life, there are countless others that are not acted on. All of you have had these ideas, not once, but often. These ideas are frightening because by their very nature they must change the world in some manner, large or small — whether it's a moon landing or an auto-flush toilet.

We fear to bring these ideas about. But once in a while, we are driven to do so. This is how one such idea came into being, teased at the periphery of my brain for some years, and then in a single moment was made flesh.

For the past five years, I have been working on "the biggest work of music drama in history" — but I didn't know for four and a half of those years.

Most musicians and fans of classical music know that "the biggest work of music drama in history" is Wagner's monumental *Ring* cycle. This work is so big that it takes four evenings to perform. It uses an orchestra of about 120 people. It tells a story that begins with the dawn of the gods and ends with the destruction of the universe. It is an icon of European, and specifically German culture. An entire town in Southern Germany, Bayreuth, is devoted to producing it and other Wagner operas, and there is a ten year waiting list for tickets.

Composing the *Ring* took decades of Wagner's life and it is one of the summits of European artistic achievement. Wagner's dream, to integrate poetry, music, and theater in a new fusion, instigated an artistic revolution that is felt not just in opera, but even in art forms that did not exist in Wagner's lifetime, such as film.

Disputing Wagner, let alone toppling him, was furthest from my mind when, in 2009, I received a request from a progressive opera company in Texas, to compose a small-scale opera. The only condition was that it would have something to do with India.

*The Silent Prince*, the work I created for this company, is adapted from *DasJati*, the collection of ten notable lives of the Buddha which is a centerpiece of Theravada Buddhism. They are ten central myths of our culture and of the entire world

Buddhist community. *The Silent Prince,* adapted from the first of the ten stories, tells of a prince whose proud father tells him to order a criminal's execution. To disobey one's father is a terrible karmic sin. To kill a man, equally sinful. Prince Temiya's deals with the moral conflict by retreating into silence.

At first the story seems far removed from our world. But today, when a child faces an intolerable dilemma and flees into an inner world, we give it a fancy name like autism or a "fugue state" or any number of fancy words. So, I wrote an opera about mythology that was also about dysfunctional families and traumatized children. It was a Buddhist parable about the contemporary world. It was, indeed, the first specifically Buddhist opera to hit the western world.

The premiere was rewarded with great reviews: the best I'd ever received. *The Silent Prince* was widely viewed as a breakthrough in my operatic career, but it was far from a project to change the world.

A few years later, we had a political upheaval in his country, and a huge international choir festival I had planned for Bangkok was about to be canceled because of travel anxiety. The Ministry of Culture said to me, "Isn't there something you could do that would use local singers, yet open a window for them to still come to Thailand?"

Thus it was that I resurrected my *Mahajanaka Symphony,* composed for the King's 60 birthday, composed in 1997 as a meditation on His Majesty's *own* meditation on the second of the ten DasJati tales — the story of a prince who braves the impossible, literally "takes up arms against a sea of troubles," and breaks through to a divine intervention. To recast this work as a drama instead of pure symphonic music, I introduced the element of narrative dance. The full length narrative ballet is a moribund art form in the west. But the Buddhist imagery gave the genre a new perspective.

I had at that point adapted two of the ten great lives of the Buddha into some kind of music-theatrical incarnation, and now I was deeply into the Jataka Tales, marvelling at their relevance to modern life, understanding they are an inheritance that constantly renews itself. I picked another jataka tale to adapt — the story of *Bhuridat*, a prince of nagas, who is captured by an unscrupulous snake charmer and forced to dance to the sound of a magic pipe for the amusement of peasants in village squares and to the enrichment of his captor.

It was then that the bolt of lightning came. I was assailed by an attack of megalomania — even hubris, because the inspiration also involved a challenge to the unchallenged gods of music.

Why stop at three operas? Why not set all ten of the Ten Lives of the Buddha to music? Why not add dance to Wagner's fusion of music, poetry and drama, and create an even richer fusion — a new art form?

A work that combined those four art forms, and consisted of ten full length productions which could be performed as a connected whole, perhaps over a seven day period, would be by definition the largest ever conceived in the history of live performance. And if there were a festival, say, every three years, in which the entire *Ten Lives of the Buddha* were performed, would that not make Thailand into a mecca for lovers of opera and dance? Would it not provide employment for singers, directors, dancers, musicians, set designers, costume designers, and interpreters — not just on a one-time basis, but for generations to come? Would not the entire fabric of the cultural universe be bent towards a part of the world not previously thought to be a world operatic center? Would the existence of this work not imprint Thailand permanently on the world's cultural community?

That, in short, is the "hubris" part of the lightning. Now, the "humility."

— *It's too big.* Well, yes, obviously it is too big. It's a new art form *and* it's ten full-length works.

— *It's too difficult.* Yes. Each of the ten stories is as complicated as the entire *Ring* cycle. Extracting the contemporary resonance from each piece and connecting them so that the entire seven-day event is clearly woven from a single skein of fabric requires holding a lot of jigsaw pieces in one's head.

— *It's too impractical.* Putting on one opera is bad enough — let alone an opera plus dance — with maybe 200-300 performers in some cases. Putting on ten means a cast of thousands. How many rehearsals?

— *I don't have the resources.* Something like this costs money, which doesn't grow on trees.

— *I am not worthy.* One looks at the giants of the past and wonders how one had the gall to think one could take them on. The weight of all that past achievement is a crushing burden.

So how does one handle the hubris? And how does one cope with the humility? Shall we start with the humility?

Is it too big? Of course it is. Is it too difficult? Of course it is. Is it impractical? Naturally. Am I unworthy to tie the shoelaces of the greats? Arguable, but without the judgment of history, let us assume that, too, is true.

I have learned that *most* of us don't actually want to *be* writers or composers. We want, rather, to *have written.* We want to jump through the hoop that is all the hard work, and fast forward to the acclaim and the money.

So first get this into your head: you are bringing this idea to fruition precisely *because* it is difficult, and complex, and daunting, expensive, and unprecedented — and that it is hard work to go through all those hoops.

When you start telling people about this idea, they will almost certainly not see what is in your head, because, let's face it, it's in *your* head, not theirs. Coupled with the skepticism of the outside world, there's also your own skepticism.

So why *should* we seize these bolts of lightning? Why *do* we go through the angst of seeing them through?

Because in the moment that lightning strikes you, you are the only person in the universe who can act. You are alone. You are the only person who can make it come to life, or consign it to the eternal void. No one can be God for all eternity, but in that singularity of spacetime, you *are* God.

One nanosecond later, you are just a mortal like anyone else.

Hubris — the Greek word for daring to challenge the fates, the gods, our own miserable destinies as specks of dust in a vast uncaring cosmos — is usually considered a bad thing, but now you're going to need it. It is indeed, the only way that you will ever be crazy enough to take the kind of chances that can change the world.

What will you gain? I regret to tell you that to hope for fame or wealth is not something that should be at the top of your list. If you look throughout history, you will see that it's usually the second person to take up a "big idea" that gets these things. The original creator often perishes in obscurity. If you're *really* lucky, you could even get burned at the stake.

If the idea is really big, don't worry about getting rewarded in this lifetime. If it happens, it's gravy.

I want to conclude with the story of a "big idea" that came simultaneously to three composers in the 1970s in Thailand — Bruce Gaston, Dnu Huntrakul, and me. We planned to revolutionize all music in Asia by creating a new fusion between Thai and Western music. Our revolution was to have its Big Bang during a music festival we planned in 1978, attended by almost all the major composers in the region.

The revolution was a bust, you see. The traditional Thai musicians I hired to play with the classical ones walked out. The papers blasted us. The Department of Fine Arts, on opening night, hid the piano and informed me that it had been scientifically determined that modern music would damage its strings.

The three of us were traumatized. We all found different ways to burn out. Bruce and Dnu went in a more commercial direction; I gave up music completely and started a new career as a science fiction writer, running away to America. The revolution was a flop.

As a new century dawned and I visited Thailand after a twenty-five year self imposed exile, I realized to my amazement that, over time, the revolution had in fact succeeded. The fusion of Thai and western musical styles was now so taken for granted that pop music and even TV commercials could freely make use of it. The revolution had permeated so profoundly into the culture that no one was even aware that a revolution had occurred, or that it had once even been necessary for a revolution to occur.

I want to tell you that this is the greatest reward that a "big idea" can ever bring. For you will have changed people's perception of the world so much that they no longer know that their perceptions were changed.

That is the ultimate revolution. The greatest ideas, from relativity to the Eroica Symphony — are facts of life. We cannot really conceive a world without them. They have been woven into the fabric of reality.

If this irony doesn't frighten you — then by all means — *be* God for a nanosecond. Grasp the lightning. Ride it. Hurl it into an unready world. I dare you.

*— end of my talk —*

So, I gave that talk over a year ago, and now I'm at the halfway point in this exploration of the central storyline of Theravada Buddhism.

The most recent opera I completed is the fourth one in the sequence. It's called *Chariot of Heaven* and its plot is ridiculously simple, having no novelistic twists and turns and no real conflict. King Nemi, last in a long line of reincarnated selves, has gradually been growing in karmic purity until he is almost ready to be born as the Buddha.

At a central moment in his life, he is summoned to heaven to preach to the gods; on his way, he stops at the entrance to hell and insists on seeing the suffering souls there.    And so this opera is a travelogue.  When Nemi reaches heaven, he remains there, teaching the *dhamma* to the gods themselves, for a span; by the time he returns to the world, much time has passed, but his people acclaim him as he appoints his son to be the last ruler of his line.

Many unstageable things happen in this opera even though there is no "conflict" per se.    For example, 84,000 generations are supposed to "pass" between two scenes of the opera, and even keeping each generation between 20-30 years means that I have to describe in music a span of two million years.    And then, how can one possible describe heaven itself in music?  Hell — not so bad, perhaps; drama and suffering have always been easier to compose    music    for    than    utter,    motionless Brahma-like stillness where nothing changes in a billion years....

The "march of time" was easy if you believe in a cyclical view of history.  I simply created ballet music that (with a little wit, I hope) suggested all the ages from cavemen through Egypt through Rome through samurai through the jazz age, blew it all up in a nuclear holocaust, then started it all up again.  It made for a fun little interlude.

But showing heaven itself is another matter. Buddhist cosmology makes it a little easier because there are many heavens, and most are so beyond imagination they do not intersect with the physical world at all.  The heaven that appears in mythology is the Tavatimsa Heaven, which is one of the lowest levels in cosmology, but is the only heaven from which divine beings can interact with the humans. Thus, the gods of Tavatimsa are more compatible with humans; they have passions and make and break promises; they even fall in love with human beings from time to time; this is, in fact, a kind of "Olympus", only the mountain is Mt. Kailasa. There are thirty-three gods who rule Tavatimsa, headed by Shakro Devanam Indra — or "Sakka" as he is called in Pali, the language of the Theravada scriptures.

This is a heaven where gods live for millions of years but are still mortal, where human history happens in the blink of an eye, so I needed to create a kind of cosmic music that expressed a kind of motion-in-stillness. For this, I created an ensemble for thirty-three separate soloists, all blending in a harmony that is always static, yet moving....

As far as I know there's never been an opera ensemble with 33 individual characters and voices weaving together at one time, so this was in fact an operatic first.

In fact it was an attempt to reproduce what I heard in my aural vision, years before, in the monastery ... the music I wrote about in *Day Thirteen: Music of the Night.*

You see, after eighteen years, the things I saw and heard are still resonating in my brain. The visions, the fantastical inner journeys, exploration of the stillness, have certainly changed me.

Have I become a "better Buddhist" because of this?   Have I become a more compassionate, levelheaded human being?   It's hard to answer.  I've never subscribed with absolute certainty to *any* system of belief because no matter how beautifully constructed they are, there's always something fuzzy, something to doubt.

All I know is that I heard things and saw things that are not part of my normal existence, and that I've been trying to communicate some of the things I experienced ever since then.  My world-view as an artist has changed irrevocably and it all ties in with *linear* and *non-linear*.

You see, as a person who was educated entirely in the western educational system, I had always seen the artistic universe as a ladder.

What this means is that if you are a composer, you stand on the shoulders of composers of the recent past — you have inherited their mantle.  That means, in my case, people like Boulez, Stockhausen ... going back further, maybe Stravinsky, Bartok, Berg ... and so on in a long line and way below, down there, near the roots of the tree, Mozart, and beyond that, the baroque, renaissance and mediaeval creators.

In this system, we are obligated to climb ever upward. The whole idea of "evolution" suggests ladders and trees and stairways to heaven.  In the 1970s, if I wrote music that was too "tonal" I would be mocked by my peers for not being progressive enough, or even selling out to the vulgar world of pop.

So, looking over my shoulder I could talk to Stockhausen or Berio and maybe shout to Schoenberg. But Lord help me if I tried to start a conversation with Brahms or Beethoven, let alone Bach ... or Tallis, Dunstable, Landini.

In my time in the temple, a different paradigm emerged. It came to me after hours of gazing into a great emptiness. Of sitting in a linked circle while a monk chanted archaic and irrelevant rules in a dead language for forty-five minutes entirely from memory. Of doing the walking meditation under a rainy sky.

Maybe, I thought, I should see the world not as a ladder, but as a circle. Maybe the great minds of the past are not linked in a long progression (Goethe's "endless chain of being") but are sitting around in a circle, equidistant from the center. Maybe Mozart and Stockhausen are the same distance from me because maybe there's no reason why time should be linear, or run in one direction only; and if that's so, I can talk to all of them once, some are *not* more distant than others.

This is the lesson that really changed *everything* for me. I no longer felt guilty about drawing a line directly from myself to, say, Monteverdi without having to pass through more recent composers. All the bold discoveries of those who went before became accessible.

And so it was that my sojourn in this other world, the experience shared by virtually all men in my country yet discovered by me only in middle age, this world both hauntingly familiar yet alien, filled with spirits and arcane jargon, became a threshold for me. I crossed over and saw the world differently; I could never go back to the old perceptions.

I cannot say that today I meditate for an hour every morning — or offer any other physical change in my life — but sometimes I do meditate. The quality of my dreams has evolved; my dreams have become more nested, one inside the other, and more lucid, and more vivid. Nine years ago I started writing them down and they too became a book I never intended to write, an open window into myself.

Now as I stand half-way through composing *DasJati,* which is already being hailed for its gigantism and monumentalism though it is not even finished, I had to stop for a time, and to fish out these journal notes I made almost two decades ago.

And the image that comes to mind most of all now is the walking meditation in the rain.

Stillness amid movement.

Last year, after the passing of the King of Thailand, I had occasion to conduct several massive performances of the Royal Anthem. One that was in the news, attended by some say as many as 300,000 people, was deemed an iconic moment, in which the entire country seemed to come together. But a week or so later I was asked to do the same thing in the town of Korat.

There were also (perhaps — no one counted) a hundred thousand people there, but this was not the huge public moment that the other was. You see, it rained. The crowd was drenched. The strings could not come out at all, because the rain would have damaged the instruments, and minutes before we were to perform, I found myself rearranging the music of the Thai Royal Anthem for brass only, reassigning the parts so the violins could stay out of the rain.

People waited a long time; many told me afterwards they did not think the orchestra would emerge at all (they had taken shelter in a little space under a monument.) But eventually I emerged. The brass instrumentalists emerged, in the pouring rain. The chorus emerged. And the other instrumentalists, determined to be part of the event, emerged as well, preparing to sing in harmony instead of play.

What happened next is that there was announcement that we would all observe nine minutes of silence to meditate on the late King Rama IX. It was something of a surprise because the rain was pouring. I had assumed they would try to make the event shorter, to get people out of the rain.

There were lit candles; people held them close, sheltering the flames with their hands. You could see people shift, uneasy at first. But suddenly magic happened. A emanated radiated from the huge royal portrait and the thousands and thousands of people seemed to breathe as one. The barriers were down between us. The grief was huge but so was the exaltation. At length, the anthem began. I wept as I conducted; I don't ever recall weeping all the way through a piece of music I was conducting. In this very public place, thousands of people were experiencing a very private sharing.

As the anthem ended, so did the rain. A wind rose up and scattered the grey clouds; a flock of birds crossed the clear sky. A Spielbergian moment of audience manipulation, except it really happened.

Thailand is a contradictory place; it is the nexus where the feudal meets the future. It's a highly materialistic society that subscribes to the least materialistic of all philosophies. It's a place of purity and corruption. Of beauty and brutality. And it's Buddhism that allows these contradictions to exist not just side by side but often within each other, so that you cannot tell which is the false shell and which the inner self. Wthin a philosophy that teaches that all truth is intrinsically illusion, I was searching for an answer to Pontius Pilate's unanswerable question.

I left Thailand when I was six months old; at 7 when I returned for the first time, it was its alienness that I loved the most. I went away again at 12; on my next return, in my mid-twenties, I began to recognize, rediscover and renew myself. But I was in Thailand for only a couple of years before reinventing myself as an American and a novelist.

This return, at the cusp of old age, is different. I'm tying up loose ends. I'm preparing for another journey. I would like to make sure that I can leave behind all ten of the *Lives of the Buddha,* and a number of works I'd had in my mind for decades. A few months ago, I picked up work on a science fiction series I abandoned thirty-three years ago. In this twilight I'm entering a time of frenetic creativity.

"In my end is my beginning." Mary Queen of Scots? T.S. Eliot? Or was it the Buddha?

# Four Noble Truths
## *Ariya Sacca*

Here's the final set of four, the center of Buddha's teaching:

*This is Suffering.*
*This is what causes Suffering.*
*Suffering can end.*
*This is the way to end it.*

When the Buddha "woke up" from his meditation beneath the tree, he preached his first sermon and these four sentences were its core.

The central idea is that suffering and existence are one — much like Einstein's matter and energy — and that the reason that existence is suffering is attachment. If attachment is an inalienable part of existence, and attachment is the cause of suffering, if follows that the idea that "suffering can end" is illogical ... unless one relinquishes attachment completely ... in which case, one would not actually exist anymore. To break the cycle, all you have to do is truly know that everything you know is an illusion.

If you truly know that all is illusion, you will automatically cease to exist and your suffering will be over. Indeed, it would never have happened, because you were never there to have it happen to you.

This is a philosophy of such elegant simplicity and such utter uncompromising purity that it would come to no surprise to realize that no Buddhists *actually* believe it. Anyone who *actually* believed it would have already gone out, like a candle.

So pretty much by definition, if you exist at all, you're not there yet. If you are even remotely conscious that you have an identity, that you are someone, you're nowhere near Nirvana. You are just another traveller, somewhere on the billion-year path.

King Nemi, the subject of the fourth of the *DasJati* stories, was consumed by a single question: Which is the surest path to enlightenment: doing good, or contemplation? Paradoxically, the answer is the latter, and his reward for reaching this conclusion is that he gets to undertake the Dantean tour of Heaven and Hell.

It took King Nemi 84,000 generations of contemplation to reach this epiphany. I'm incomparably more venal than King Nemi, so I cut a few corners.

I didn't take the slow train. I took the Nirvana

Express and I ended up where I began.
But I learned that *all* endings are beginnings.
                     — *Bangkok, 2001-2018*

# About the Author

Once referred to by the International Herald Tribune as "the most well-known expatriate Thai in the world," Somtow Sucharitkul is no longer an expatriate, since he has returned to Thailand after five decades of wandering the world. He is best known as an award-winning novelist and a composer of operas.

Born in Bangkok, Somtow grew up in Europe and was educated at Eton and Cambridge. His first career was in music and in the 1970s he acquired a reputation as a revolutionary composer, the first to combine Thai and Western instruments in radical new sonorities. Conditions in the arts in the region at the time proved so traumatic for the young composer that he suffered a major burnout,

emigrated to the United States, and reinvented
himself as a novelist.

His earliest novels were in the science fiction
field but he soon began to cross into other genres. In

his 1984 novel *Vampire Junction,* he injected a new literary inventiveness into the horror genre, in the words of Robert Bloch, author of *Psycho,* "skilfully combining the styles of Stephen King, William Burroughs, and the author of the Revelation to John." *Vampire Junction* was voted one of the forty all-time greatest horror books by the Horror Writers' Association, joining established classics like *Frankenstein* and *Dracula.*

In the 1990s Somtow became increasingly identified as a uniquely Asian writer with novels such as the semi-autobiographical *Jasmine Nights.* He won the World Fantasy Award, the highest accolade given in the world of fantastic literature, for his novella *The Bird Catcher.* His fifty-three books have sold about two million copies world-wide.After becoming a Buddhist monk for a period in 2001, Somtow decided to refocus his attention on the country of his birth, founding Bangkok's first international opera company and returning to music, where he again reinvented himself, this time as a neo-Asian neo-Romantic composer. The Norwegian government commissioned his song cycle *Songs Before Dawn* for the 100th Anniversary of the Nobel Peace Prize, and he composed at the request of the government of Thailand his *Requiem: In Memoriam 9/11* which was dedicated to the victims of the 9/11 tragedy.

According to London's Opera magazine, "in just five years, Somtow has made Bangkok into the operatic hub of Southeast Asia." His operas on Thai themes, *Madana, Mae Naak, Ayodhya*, and *The Silent Prince* have been well received by international critics. His most recent operas, the Japanese inspired *Dan no Ura* and the fantasy opera *The Snow Dragon,* have gained him acceptance as "one of the most intriguing of contemporary opera com-posers" (Auditorium Magazine). He has recently embarked on a ten-opera cycle, *DasJati — Ten Lives of the Buddha* - which when completed will be the classical music work with the largest time span and scope in history.

He is increasingly in demand as a conductor specializing in opera and in the late-romantic composers like Mahler. His repertoire runs the entire gamut from Monteverdi to Wagner. His work has been especially lauded for its stylistic authenticity and its lyricism. He has received the "Golden W" from the International Wagner Society. The orchestra he founded in Bangkok, the Siam Philharmonic, mounted the first complete Mahler cycle in the region.

Somtow's current project, the Siam Sinfonietta, is a youth orchestra he founded five years ago, using a new educational method he pioneered and which is now among the most acclaimed youth orchestras world-wide, receiving standing ovations in Carnegie Hall, The Konzerthaus in Berlin, Disney Hall, the Musikverein in Vienna, and many other venues around the world.

He is the first recipient of Thailand's "Distinguished Silpathorn" award, given for an artist who has made and continues to make a major impact on the region's culture, from Thailand's Ministry of Culture.

He is the first Asian (and only the second composer after Hans Werner Henze) to receive the Europa Kultur-Forum's European Cultural Achievement Award.

# Books by S.P. Somtow

**General Fiction**
*The Shattered Horse*
*Jasmine Nights*
*Forgetting Places*
*The Other City of Angels (Bluebeard's Castle)*
*The Stone Buddha's Tears*

**Dark Fantasy**
The Timmy Valentine Series:
     *Vampire Junction*
     *Valentine*
     *Vanitas*
*Vampire Junction Special Edition*
*Moon Dance*
*Darker Angels*
*The Vampire's Beautiful Daughter*

**Science Fiction**
*Starship & Haiku*
*Mallworld*
*The Ultimate Mallworld*
*The Ultimate, Ultimate, Ultimate Mallworld*

Chronicles of the High Inquest:
  *Light on the Sound*
  *The Darkling Wind*
  *The Throne of Madness*
  *Utopia Hunters*
*Chroniques de l'Inquisition - Volume 1* (omnibus)
*Chroniques de l'Inquisition - Volume 2* (omnibus)
*Inquestor Tales One: The Singing Moons*
*Inquestor Tales Two: A Woman Cloaked in Shadow*
*Inquestor Tales Three: The Child Collector*

The Aquiliad Series:
  *Aquila in the New World*
  *Aquila and the Iron Horse*
  *Aquila and the Sphinx*

**Fantasy**
The Riverrun Trilogy:
  *Riverrun*
  *Armorica*
  *Yestern*
*The Riverrun Trilogy* (omnibus)
*The Fallen Country Wizard's Apprentice*
*The Snow Dragon* (omnibus)


**Media Tie-in**
*The Alien Swordmaster*
*Symphony of Terror*
*The Crow - Temple of Night*
*Star Trek: Do Comets Dream?*

**Chapbooks**
*Fiddling for Waterbuffaloes*
*I Wake from a Dream of a Drowned Star City*

*A Lap Dance with the Lobster Lady*
*Compassion — Two Perspectives*

## Libretti
*Mae Naak*
*Ayodhya*
*Madana*
*Dan no Ura*
*Helena Citronova*
*The Snow Dragon*
Dasjati:
        *Temiya - The Silent Prince*
        *Sama - The Faithful Son*
        *Bhuridat - The Dragon Lord*
        *Mahosadha - Architect of Dreams*
        *Nemiraj - Chariot of Heaven*

## Collections
*My Cold Mad Father* (in press)
*Fire from the Wine Dark Sea*
*Chui Chai* (Thai)
*Nova* (Thai)
*The Pavilion of Frozen Women*
*Dragon's Fin Soup*
*Tagging the Moon*
*Face of Death* (Thai)
*Other Edens*
*S.P. Somtow's The Great Tales* (Thai)
*Terror Nova* (in press)
*Terror Antiqua* (in press)

## Essays, Poetry and Miscellanies
*Opus Fifty*
*A Certain Slant of "I"* (in press)
*Sonnets about Serial Killers*

*Opera East*
*Victory in Vienna* (ed.)
*Three Continents* (ed.)
*Nirvana Express*
*Caravaggio x 2*
*The Maestro's Noctuary*